CW00631736

The
Centrist Dad
Handbook

The Centrist Dad Handbook

Jason Hazeley &
Nico Tatarowicz

BLOOMSBURY
LONDON · OXFORD · NEW YORK · NEW DELHI · SYDNEY

BLOOMSBURY PUBLISHING
Bloomsbury Publishing Plc
50 Bedford Square, London, WC1B 3DP, UK
29 Earlsfort Terrace, Dublin 2, Ireland

BLOOMSBURY, BLOOMSBURY PUBLISHING and the Diana logo
are trademarks of Bloomsbury Publishing Plc

First published in Great Britain 2024

A catalogue record for this book is available from the British Library

ISBN: HB: 978-1-5266-8199-7; eBook: 978-1-5266-8195-9;
ePDF: 978-1-5266-8196-6

2 4 6 8 10 9 7 5 3 1

Typeset by Ed Pickford

Printed and bound in Great Britain by CPI Group (UK) Ltd,
Croydon CR0 4YY

To find out more about our authors and books visit
www.bloomsbury.com and sign up for our newsletters

Contents

Look at the state of him.

Centrist Dads:
An Introduction

You have in your hands *The Centrist Dad Handbook.*

But why?

You may have been given this book as a gift by someone who suspects that you are a Centrist Dad. Don't be alarmed: this is not a social death sentence, and may even turn out to be a sign of affection.

You may have bought it yourself because you know you are a Centrist Dad and want to deepen your self-knowledge. Well done you. You have taken responsibility for who and what you are.

If, however, you are not yet sure if you are a Centrist Dad, suspend your judgement until you have finished the book. If you are still in doubt then, you are, frankly, on your own. After all, you are a fully grown adult (presumably: if you are a child buying a book about Centrist Dads then you may have bigger problems).

But should you already feel a pang of self-recognition at the idea that you are now in a social group that includes Adrian Chiles, Brompton Bicycles and the gilet, remember to think kindly of yourself, because being a Centrist Dad is nothing to be *that* embarrassed about. The authors themselves have had to come to terms with this and have accepted their fate as members of a cultural subset who will forever have one cheek – uncomfortably, but sensibly – on either side of the fence. (Although one of them refuses to give up his National Trust membership and the other still thinks it's OK to have seven different types of mustard in the fridge.)

Who is Centrist Dad?

You may not have given him much thought until recently, but Centrist Dad has always been around, modestly trying to save the world one sensible decision at a time and respectfully making sure everybody knows about it.

You may have seen him at the recycling centre with colour-coded bags of separated rubbish nestling in the boot of his default hatchback. Or perhaps in a café, peering over a copy of the *Guardian*, *The Times* or both, but on alternate days. He is likely to be still wearing a cycling helmet on his train to work, which makes total sense to him because it is going faster than he can cycle. At home he listens to 6 Music (with the volume at 3) on a duck-egg blue pleather Roberts Revival radio.

In winter, he prepares his weekly casseroles in a Le Creuset, but one that he got from Keech Hospice Care, because what matters most to him is helping to give people who haven't had much for all of their lives a dignified ending via the purchase of discarded and now insanely cheap yet high-quality kitchenware.

Centrist Dad is the man who relaxes by watching major football matches at home (with the TV moved into the conservatory) with no more than eight friends, none of whom cry at the end when their team inevitably loses on penalties, because it's the only football match any of them have watched for four years. Yet at parties he is also the hero who presses pause if a Smiths song comes on the Bluetooth speaker, so he can conduct a brief Smiths Election that

It's not easy being a conscientious objector to the culture wars but there's nothing an oat milk latte can't fix.

takes into account everyone's current views on Morrissey before just putting on some Moby so everyone can relax.

In times gone by, he may very well have been seen politely manning a trestle table for the SDP outside KwikSave. Nowadays he is very likely indeed to be the co-host of a 'refreshing' weekly political podcast, which takes the form of a sparring session between two bloody good straight-talking (and straight) male eggs who have put aside their tiny differences to try and dampen the flames of the issues of the day. They achieve this by compromising all the heat out of their own thinly veiled opinions until they are like tepid gruel – all the while being so hideously agreeable to each other that you almost expect them to fuck on mic.

Got him now? Good.

What is Centrism?

Centrism is generally understood to be a lack of political leaning in either direction that can result in the two main parties of a developed country becoming so close together in ideology that one could actually go cross-eyed deciding who to vote for. But there is *far* more to centrism than just politics.

Both as a universe and a system of thinking, centrism is as infinite as it is wafer thin, and the nearer the nucleus of this slender paradigm one gets, the more breathtakingly bland it becomes. It is neither macro nor micro, which means it will one day probably be termed *mecro*.* It's like an illusion that nobody can be bothered to see; a Möbius strip made out of pliable bloke.

The paradox of the centriverse is that the middle of the middle of the middle is so painfully safe and non-committal that is almost impossible to conceive of it at all. And, in that context, centrism can safely be described as a scientific and philosophical miracle. Just … quite a boring one that nobody really marvels at. Because why would you?

Does Centrist Dad Have to be a Dad? Does He Even Have to be a He?

No, but he does have to think like one. Centrist Dadism can best be described as a state of mind. An attitude. A way of life. A commitment to being a mild but well-meaning pain in the arse for all of eternity. With that in mind, it

---

* You read it here first.

is acceptable to point it out in others where it is seen growing in unusual places. To that end, the phrase 'Alright, Centrist Dad!' may be deployed in much the same way people say, 'OK, boomer!'

Centrist Dadness lives in the air, like radio waves, dead skin and wasps, and does not require the fertilisation of any sort of egg in order to be activated. The truth is that its power lies in the reassuring comfort of its ways. It hides in the gentle siren call of the 40 per cent discounted North Face fleece luring him towards the rocky shelves of Mountain Warehouse — and in the deep, erotic desire to store cheese in a locking airtight container while singing along to 'Losing My Religion' on Heart 90s. These are traits that can take hold of anyone if they do not remain vigilant against the hazy glory of playing it safe. Siring an actual child and then taking it to karate on a Tuesday evening is only a very small part of that.

So a practising Centrist Dad is absolutely *not* required to have reproduced. He needn't have been jogging with a Bugaboo Fox 5 while making business calls, or attended a PTA meeting in his gym gear on his way to squash.

He might be an uncle. A teacher. A friend. He could just be a man on a train with a Dell laptop bag frowning into an iPhone that refuses to let go of him.

He doesn't even need to be a *he* at all. Anyone can find they have become Centrist Dad if they spend long enough in his company. After all, reasonableness and moral certainty can be intoxicating – even contagious – and for that reason it pays for those around him to stay alert to their own susceptibility to straying into the middle lane. For example, after a long day with any Centrist Dad, one is recommended to take an ice bath well away from the house, perhaps also using a Neti Pot to empty one's head. It might even be a good idea to listen to *Never Mind The Bollocks* by the Sex Pistols to try and get back in contact with one's own thoughts and emotions.

The number one Centrist Dad trait to look out for in the wild is a kind of casual presentation of being right about absolutely any point on any subject throughout history by dint of being vague and open-ended. In other words, he may use a lot of words but say not very much at all while numbing everyone into submission. This usually happens while everyone else in the conversation tears their hair out until finally giving up. It is important to note at such times that Centrist Dad *can't see* how being über-reasonable 100 per cent of the time is difficult for those around him. This is because he has the self-awareness of a shaggy dog who has just got out of a muddy lake next to a bride in a sparkling white wedding dress.

But we mustn't judge him too harshly. He is, after all, usually trying (much too hard) to do the right thing, and very rarely sets out to offend anyone. If he wants to help to calm down a situation he has caused by being so utterly pleased with his position, Centrist Dad could try techniques like winding his fucking neck in now and again, or choosing an actual opinion once in a sodding while.

Although there is plenty of debate surrounding certain difficulties in Centrist Dad's character (for example, a level of certainty only usually displayed by ancient gods), it is worth clearly stating that Centrist Dadism does not appear anywhere on the DSM–5 list of recognised personality disorders. However, research is continuing and there are already a handful of pressure groups that are trying to change this because they find their own fathers, husbands, bosses and tennis doubles partners so blood-curdlingly insufferable.

All that being said, Centrist Dad is *stuck with himself* just as unfortunately as his fellow citizens and family are, and all he can really do is try as best he can to accurately identify himself and his traits so that he can alert others to his condition before any culture wars, political grandstanding or conversations about *almost anything at all* break out.

This can be viewed much in the same way that a person with a stinking cold might warn people off giving them a snuggle, or how the gluten intolerant make sure that waiters, chefs and everybody within four miles knows that they have bravely forgone the entire universe of wheat, and that they must now be tip-toed around like an unexploded World War II bomb.

The Centrist Dad
Hall of Fame

Centrist Dad is everywhere. He's at the school gate, he's in the pub, he's in the gym, he's in the office; he's opposite you on the train, he's next to you at the lights (on a bike, obviously), he's in front of you in the supermarket queue; he's in your book group, your five-a-side *and* your quiz team.

But he's also beaming down at you from billboards and chuntering away on nine of the top ten podcasts and being that nice guy on the TV and the radio – because there are plenty of famous Centrist Dads. There's even one behind the door of 10 Downing Street now. Which is sort of as exciting as it isn't. More of a relief, like when you check if there's Parmesan in the fridge halfway through cooking a bolognese, and there is.

There was a vintage Centrist Dad managing the England football team with more overall success than anyone else literally *ever* until the day after Euro 2024, which England had been in with a chance of actually winning until five minutes before the end of the whole tournament. His name was **Gareth Southgate** and the managing bit was the bit he was good at. (Which was just as well, because that was the bit he was *supposed* to be good at or he'd have been deemed rubbish and someone would have Photoshopped a vegetable onto his face in a tabloid and he'd have been sacked because there is no comeback from the turnip-head treatment.) During his tenure Gareth was booed and cheered, sometimes by the same bellends in the crowd during the same game. Which he

Winning is too vulgar for a Centrist like Gareth Southgate, so he sticks to nearly winning.

usually won. And he managed it all like some sort of middle-management manager but with more managerial skills. And then he resigned quietly, having modernised the entire culture of the England football team, which used to be made of drinking games and sulking and car-crashes and now is the shape of semi-finals and finals, and rainbow armbands and meritocratic youth-driven diversity instead. Not bad for a centrist central defender from Watford.

Another high achiever with a patina of ordinariness is Professor **Brian Cox**. He was the keyboard player in New Labour, the most successful centrist movement of all time. Now he stares misty-eyed at the universe on our screens, reminding us how humble we all are, and how none of us will ever have teeth as beautiful as his.

And remember **Nick Clegg**? He was briefly the poster boy for centrism, when his political party, the resolutely centrist Liberal Democrats, were riding high in the polls before the 2010 general election. That was before Nick 'I Agree With Nick' Clegg took up the invitation to form a coalition government with the Conservatives, effectively shitting his entire reputation away. When he lost his seat in 2017, he took a job at Facebook, thereby shitting his chance at restoring his reputation away too. Whether he is still a centrist is unclear, because it's hidden under a heaving mound of shit (although having escaped to California to make millions of dollars, he may not be too bothered about that).

Elsewhere in the political biosphere, there are the **Miliband Brothers**. David 'Former Future Labour Leader' Miliband, the thinking man's thinking man, put aside his party ambitions when Ed 'You've Got the Wrong' Miliband became Labour leader in 2010. Both are the sons of a Marxist academic, but both are resolutely centrist. Indeed, it is possible to argue that the reason Ed lost the 2015 general election is the same reason David lost the Labour leadership election: because they were *too reasonable*. In retrospect, Ed Miliband should have taken that bacon sandwich and lobbed it at David Cameron. It could have been the long-awaited sequel to John Prescott clouting the bloke who egged him.*

Facing Ed from the other side of the House of Commons back when he was on the front bench was **George Osborne**. Osborne is a

---

* According to well-sourced rumours, the Artificial Intelligence faculty at Berkeley devised a third brother, Jonathan Miliband 3000MXC, who was ultra-centrist but with none of the flaws of Ed and David. Unfortunately, he was so hypersensible that three of the team developing him died of boredom.

slippery centrist. For a start, George is not his name. He's Gideon. And for another thing, he devised 'austerity', which is also not its real name. It's 'national impoverishment'. And yet, he left politics, became the editor of a disproportionately important newspaper and started a podcast with Balls. And they both sound like Centrist Dads. But are they? It is, of course, possible that Osborne has had a conversion from venal capitalist to benign centrist – but it's just as plausible that he spotted the Centrist Dad bandwagon rolling through town and vaulted onto it. His fellow podcaster was always closer to the centre than the left, so Balls didn't roll far on that journey. Plus, he burnished his Centrist Dad reputation by cronking around to 'Gangnam Style' on *Strictly Come Dancing*. And Centrist Dad publicly Dad Dancing is fully loaded Dad.

Stewart Lee seems an unusual name to add to the list, leaning as he does to the left, but he's very much a Centrist Dad. With his long, opinionated, softly spoken routines, he's what every Centrist Dad longs to be: actually funny.

But the big beasts are in the opinionated-but-not-for-a-laugh zone.

James O'Brien, the LBC host and patron saint of reason, is at the top table of Centrist Dads. He's the closest the atheist community gets to a hospital chaplain: always articulate, always compassionate, and with a nice tidy beard and a reassuring bedside manner which comforts the patient. (Not all his 'patients' – listeners – are ill, we are legally obliged to point out. But let's face it: life is hard.)

O'Brien's Jedi-like level of anger absorption is the closest thing to centrist magic. He disarms his irate callers with the one tool they're for some reason not expecting: *he asks them what they mean.* And when he does, their positions fall to bits so comprehensively that they end up sounding like a kid who's said they left their homework on the moon.

O'Brien could charm the strings off a banjo – which, to be fair, sounds like a good idea. (Has anyone tried him on bagpipes?) He's smart and mellow and his books – *How To Be Right, How Not To Be Wrong, How To Be Not Not Right, How Not To Be Not Wrong, How Not To Not Be Not Not Right* and the other one – are like honey drizzled over Centrist Dad's tired and confuzzled brain. James O'Brien is a spa weekend for Centrist Dad's mind, and at a fraction of the cost. Long may he purr.

Next up: Batman and Rorin. No, that isn't a typo: it's a pun which doesn't work. Batman, in this instance, is **Alastair Campbell**, Tony

'Centrist Dad' Blair's right-hand man for many years, and architect of the Downing Street press operation that gave us Sure Start, the minimum wage and the Iraq war.[*]

Campbell, now appearing in your ears about 45 times a week on his podcast *The Rest is Politics* and at many, many public appearances and festivals – who knows? He might well be in one of your cupboards next time you open it – is an apparently unstoppable and unavoidable opinion hydrant. He's thought about everything, and weighed it all in the balance, and has plenty to say about it. He's a national treasure.[**]

His co-host on *The Rest is Politics* is Rory Stewart, the Rorin of the duo. Stewart, like Campbell, is a Scot. Yet the two of them don't want to kill each other and they're actually very good at mowing the lawn on each other's common ground. They respect it, tend it, and re-seed it where necessary.

But Stewart, like Campbell, is an iconoclast in his own right. He likes the occasional bit of unusual, like walking across Afghanistan alone three months after 9/11, or admitting, while running to be leader of the Conservative party,

---

[*] Two out of three ain't bad.
[**] [Citation needed]

to having smoked opium at an Iranian wedding – or, weirdest of all, endorsing the bananas Brexit blowhard David Davis.

As a pair, they are an anomaly: two bagpiping politicos from different sides of the divide who have built up an enormous following based on mild disagreement. It doesn't sound like a recipe for success. But the same is true of Mr Blobby. And carpaccio. And the execrable 'Shaddap You Face', and that was a number one single in nine countries.*

Then there's the biggest Centrist Dad of them all: **Gary Lineker**. The silver-tongued, silver-haired silverback of the Centrist Dad tribe.

Lineker has all the bases of Centrist Dad covered.** He not only represents centrism – he also represents football, liberalism and … potatoes.

Imagine representing potatoes. Where would you start? How can you excuse the bulky carb catastrophe that is the spud? Especially in this

---

* Centrist Dad loves a bit of trivia like this. He can take it to the pub.

** This is a baseball metaphor. Centrist Dad loves baseball metaphors. He says 'step up to the plate' and 'curveball' and 'out of leftfield' and 'ballpark figure' and 'heavy hitter' and 'spitball' and 'touch base' and 'knock it out of the park', even though, like all Brits, he finds the game itself utterly incomprehensible.

age of carb-dodging. You should be endorsing the asparagus or the pecan or the boiled egg. But Lineker – who's always been in fantastic shape – has stuck his flag in the potato and claimed it as his own.

As a Leicester lad, he's proud to support the city's other great export: Walkers crisps. This makes him One of the Good Guys. Even though no-one can claim that crisps are good for you, this has never blighted Lineker's reputation. He's the Centrist Dad that all Centrist Dads look up to. Lineker is who they all want to be: a handsome, witty, successful liberal who's brilliant at football with a lifetime's supply of free crisps. Although his is a bit of a cautionary tale, of which more later.

These are the Centrist Dad stars. And this is their sensible, moderate firmament.

Our New Centrist Overlord

Lineker might be the Centrist Dads' Centrist Dad, and able to bag the fan trophy without challenge, but when it comes to clout, one Centrist Dad has it in popularly mandated spades: Sir Keir Starmer, the Prime Minister of the United Kingdom of Great Britain and Northern Ireland.

Centrist Dad could never have dreamed of having one of his kind behind the door of No. 10. He might as well have dreamed of inheriting Dermot O'Leary's salary. Or Guy Garvey's vinyl collection. But this is where Centrist Dad is now – in charge. How to explain this?

By the summer of 2024 (which lasted about 48 hours), Britain was ready for change, but instead of hankering for something radical, it went for something somehow even more radical: the profoundly unradical. A safe pair of hands so safe that it might as well have had 100 fingers and hi-vis gloves.

Keir Starmer is known for being methodical, careful and pragmatic. In other words, boring. But once you examine and scrutinise the detail of his centrism, it's fascinating (sort of). It reaches far and wide and still manages to remain welded stiffly to the middle.

Starmer's centrism is rock solid. For every yin, he has a yang.

He came from a working-class household, but in a middle-class area. As a young lad, he was a bit of a bruiser, but also played the flute. He had a highly paid career as a barrister but did half the work *pro bono*. He's a master of both sides. In the run-up to the 2024 general election,

Even the highest ranking Centrist Dad never leaves home without a cagoule.

his ten pledges were carefully balanced by his quietly unpledging half of them. So, for instance, defending free movement became not having free movement, and abolition of the House of Lords became adding more peers to the House of Lords.

Some would call this political genius. Others would call it spinelessness. The clever part is, it's neither: it's just centrism, red and blue in tooth and claw.

Starmer is the most powerful Centrist Dad in the UK. He has co-opted centrism and made it his superpower. It's no accident that superheroes tend to have red and blue clothing – Starmer is centrism's first superhero. He may even represent the beginnings of a franchise called the Centrist Dad Universe, with films and lunchboxes and dollies. There are many years of his prime ministry to come, and plenty of opportunity for him to make his paternal centrism one of the UK's greatest national characteristics, along with scotch eggs and shit weather.

Translating Centrist Dad

Centrist Dad has finely honed his ability to answer questions without taking sides or revealing anything.* It's a constant psychological balancing act, but one he can now pull off with ease. But his equivocal replies may make what he says unclear, or in need of translation for those of a less centrist disposition. So this basic glossary should come in helpful.

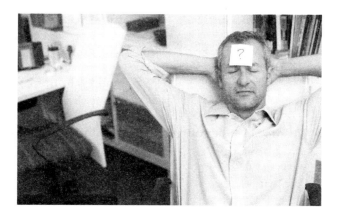

---

* He really should play more poker: although, see the chapter on Games for why he doesn't.

CENTRIST DAD	ENGLISH
'Can I come back to you on that?'	'I'll give it some thought'
'I'll give it some thought'	'Interesting idea'
'Interesting idea'	'Sounds good'
'Sounds good'	'Shouldn't be a problem'
'Shouldn't be a problem'	'That's one option'
'That's one option'	'What else you got?'
'What else you got?'	'Go on...'
'Go on...'	'We should talk more about this'
'We should talk more about this'	'Let me sleep on it'
'Let me sleep on it'	'That should be fine'
'That should be fine'	'That could work'
'That could work'	'Hmm'

CENTRIST DAD	ENGLISH
'Hmm'	'How do you mean?'
'How do you mean?'	'Is that right?'
'Is that right?'	'Wow, are you sure?'
'Wow, are you sure?'	'What do you think?
'What do you think?'	'I know, right?'
'I know, right?'	'Both sides have their merits'
'Both sides have their merits'	'Uh-huh'
'Uh-huh'	'Riiiight'
'Riiiight'	'Good point'
'Good point'	'Let's take this offline'
'Let's take this offline'	'I have some thoughts'
'I have some thoughts'	'Good question'

CENTRIST DAD	ENGLISH
'Good question'	'Funny you should ask that'
'Funny you should ask that'	'Could go either way'
'Could go either way'	'Let's see, shall we?'
'Let's see, shall we?'	'Wouldn't you like to know?'
'Wouldn't you like to know?'	'Ah, that old chestnut'
'Ah, that old chestnut'	'Not the first time I've been asked'
'Not the first time I've been asked'	'I thought you might say that'
'I thought you might say that'	'Really sorry, but I don't have time for this just now'
'Really sorry, but I don't have time for this just now'	'Can I come back to you on that?'

These are literal, textual translations, of course. The other interpretation is subtextual. And the subtextual translations of the above look like this.

CENTRIST DAD	ENGLISH
'Can I come back to you on that?'	'Please don't ask me to make a decision'
'I'll give it some thought'	'Please don't ask me to make a decision'
'Interesting idea'	'Please don't ask me to make a decision'
'Sounds good'	'Please don't ask me to make a decision'

And so on.

The Centrist Dad Quiz

Being a Centrist Dad is all about balance, as we've seen: which means that the Dad part of being a Centrist Dad is exactly as important as the Centrist part. Centrist Dad loves his kids. He wants nothing more than for them to be the very best versions of themselves they can. Which, of course, means them having exactly the same opinions as him. But this is also true of dads who are members of Momentum or Reform. So how does Centrist Dad rise above the partisan dads?

The most appropriate word for his parenting style from Centrist Dad's point of view would be 'involved', though the children themselves might come to view his 'involvement' in similar terms to how the citizens of communist-era East Berlin used to view the reassuring 'involvement' of the Stasi officer in their loft.

Centrist Dad trying to persuade Oscar that an ex-box is as good as an Xbox.

Of course, his methods of influence, shall we say, are far less severe than the average totalitarian regime. Openness, self-expression and exposure to lots of interesting new forms of inspiration, entertainment and education are all actively encouraged. It's just that they are encouraged via a moral vetting system that makes a Norton 360 Deluxe Firewall look like a sheet of newspaper over a smashed car window.

This is understandable in today's wild west world of 24-hour internet access, online gaming and Andrew fucking Tate, but worrying so much about what is entering his progeny's precious little heads will drive him up the wall if he's not careful.

And while it's kind of cool that he wants to make absolutely sure that the lights of his life understand the importance that non-violent male role models, carbon neutrality and diligent problem solving are going to hold in their futures, he also understands that at some point they *must* also watch *Die Hard* with him until well after midnight on Christmas Eve whilst shovelling crisps and Haribo down their gullets.

So how can you tell he's a *bona fide* Centrist Dad? This simple questionnaire will help, but if it's still too complicated for you, the correct answers are in **bold**.

WHERE DOES HE SEND HIS KIDS TO SCHOOL?

- Somewhere charmingly far away like Hong Kong

- A boarding school that looks like a CGI castle
- **The local academy, because they've got excellent pastoral outreach**

HOW DOES HE REMEMBER HIS KIDS' BIRTHDAYS?

- His PA has it in his calendar, which he has never once checked himself
- It's in his ★★★DONOTFORGET.xlsx spreadsheet
- **He could never forget the most humbling days of his life (at least, not since he got Google Calendar)**

WHAT WAS HIS SIGNATURE DISH FOR THE KIDS WHEN THEY WERE SMALL?

- Pom-Bears
- Kedgeree, like his great-grandfather used to insist upon
- **Pasta with pesto, 16 times per week**

WHAT DOES HE DO IN THE DADS' RACE AT SPORTS DAY?

- Win at all costs
- Stand by the sidelines shaking his head at the oiks
- **Take part. Badly**

DOES HE SPEND ENOUGH QUALITY TIME WITH HIS KIDS?

- Not if there's a nice comfy conference hotel he can elope to
- Does watching *Kung Fu Panda 4* on a loop for six months count?
- **He tries to, but you can only take them to the recycling centre so many times before someone falls into a skip**

WHAT DOES HE WANT HIS KIDS TO BE WHEN THEY'RE OLDER?

- Influential
- Wealthy

- **Able to make a decent tapenade from memory**

HOW DOES HE SHOW HIS KIDS AFFECTION?

- By letting them come home from school the odd weekend
- He calls them by their favourite superhero's name
- **Hugs, but only if they're OK with that, and not in front of their friends**

HOW DOES HE STOP THEM FROM ARGUING WHEN THEY'RE LITTLE?

- Threaten them with a fly swat
- Lock them out of the house in the howling wind
- **Ask them to evaluate the choices they're making during a six-hour bonding exercise**

WHAT WOULD HE DO IF ONE OF THEM SAID THEY WERE GOING TO VOTE FOR THE BNP?

- Disown them
- Threaten to join the BNP to put them off the idea
- **Say nothing, but spend the next three months in therapy talking about it**

WHAT DOES HE READ TO THEM AT STORY TIME?

- *The Communist Manifesto For Kids*
- Ayn Rand's *Bedtime Objectivism*
- **Miffy, because *you* try finding the controversy in a colourless Dutch rabbit**

WHO DOES HE REACH OUT TO FOR PARENTAL SUPPORT?

- Sorry, I don't understand the question
- discipline.org

- **Other members of the amazing Centrist Dad community (i.e., cyclists)**

HOW DOES HE TEACH THEM TO RIDE A BIKE?

- By getting them stabilisers
- By getting them one of those ones without pedals
- **By using a rich variety of metaphorical scenarios about balance**

HOW IS CENTRIST DAD A ROLE MODEL TO HIS KIDS?

- He can do the whole alphabet in one burp
- He ignores them half the time so they won't get too needy
- **He always takes both their sides, even if they're both wrong – it's just easier**

WHAT DOES HE ASK FOR AT CHRISTMAS?

- Whisky
- Forgiveness
- **Socks, without a hint of irony**

WHO DOES HE WANT HIS KIDS TO ADMIRE?

- Jordan B. Peterson
- Jeremy B. Corbyn
- **BBC Four**

Centrist Dad's Games

Living in an actual family with a Centrist Dad may occasionally be skyscrapingly annoying – for instance, when he somehow wins an argument that hasn't even started by announcing he simply won't be having it at all and then going outside to his shed. A masterful move. But it could also be much, much worse.

Centrist Dad is a person who wants the best for everyone, who is (theoretically) dedicated to listening to everyone's points of view and whose personality is carefully designed around not harming a fly. Which is all very admirable in theory, but can be fucking unbearable for everyone in any given room (except for the fly).

But what happens when it is time for him to let his hair down? What if, for instance, someone suggests (deep breath) we *all do something fun together?* Sounds simple enough, but

high in Centrist Dad's terrifying matrix of
eventualities is the worry that everyone has
a very different idea of what fun actually *is*.
In many families, these are the circumstances
in which board games can break out, which
usually means everyone privately relishing the
opportunity to thrash, argue with, sabotage,
pinch and shit on each other with pernicious
abandon.

Such barbarism will not stand under Centrist
Dad's roof. He doesn't like dividing his loved
ones into winners and losers and fears nothing
more than a sudden kink in the balanced
domestic social structure when, for example,
Nathan (9) has just accrued a hotel chain at the
expense of his sister Molly (12), who is now
seething in prison.

Centrist Dad, rather sweetly and very inac-
curately, sees his whole family as better than
this, which of course just makes them want
to eviscerate him at any available opportunity
so they can laugh at him trying to swallow his
anger like a goose on a foie gras farm.

Of course, Centrist Dad is no fool and knows
very well how to identify the banana skins that
are laid out for him by his loved ones to slip
up on in the name of fun. Like an after-dinner
Indiana Jones, he steps around the options that

awaken too much of the wrong kind of competition in his tribe. This is why the corridor of board and parlour games that he can bear to take part in is so alarmingly thin and so carefully policed.

So, what family fun passes the Centrist Dad sniff test?

Well firstly, absolutely nothing fun is getting through the door that wasn't bought during a trip to Waterstones alongside books for various members of the family. To Centrist Dad, a trip to Waterstones is the equivalent of an intellectual sheep-dip for those with whom he shares his living environment. The general rule of thumb is that all members of the household must read broadly, widely and quietly, lest they be charged with not having the requisite background information to form an opinion on anything at all.

Once several recent and thoughtful non-fiction bestsellers have been obtained, choosing a game from the hallowed bookshop carries the same sentiment as being allowed a dessert after one has eaten one's vegetables. This is because more than anything, Centrist Dad feels that games are not to be enjoyed, or won, they are to *prove that the whole family and his chosen friends are as clever and sophisticated as he is.*

Counterfeit, hooky or similar-looking, less fully realised versions of prestige board games bought from more irresponsible-sounding outlets like WHSmith and (God forbid) TK Maxx are simply *not permissible.* If there happens to be a cartoon on the box, it is likely to be trodden flat and put in the recycling or left in a charity shop doorway before the box has even been unsealed.

Whichever game does make it home, Centrist Dad will present as a grudging participant in it because he cannot allow himself to stir the silt of his deeply buried competitive side. This is the reason that Centrist Dad will try to delay

The Centrist sweet spot: nobody can win or lose a jigsaw.

all board-game playing until such a time as the whole family is in a busy gastropub where they cannot humiliate themselves and each other before storming off in a monolithic rage to their bedrooms.

Firstly, let's deal with the games that Centrist Dad would not be seen dead playing and that no one should attempt to play with him.

Games He's Not on Board With

TRIVIAL PURSUIT

This is possibly the world's most famous family fun game, but its very title makes it a non-starter for Centrist Dad, as his whole ethos is built around only pursuing pursuits that are, at the very least, *meaningful* and that ideally have a sort of performatively wholesome and dutiful payoff. Sitting around causing your loved ones to feel deeply inferior for not knowing the Latin name for a courgette is absolutely not that. Hard pass.

CHARADES

Centrist Dad has nothing against charades *in theory*. The problems start when he has to decide what to actually act out in front of his audience. He needs his references to be demonstrative of his cultured aura, which often leads to excruciatingly long, buzz-killing attempts to mime clever clogs books like *The Unbearable Lightness of Being* to a row of agonised and blank faces who just wanted to smash four bottles of wine with a Spotify playlist plonking along in the background. Avoid.

MONOPOLY

Sadly this one is also a no-go area for Centrist Dad, due largely to the moral implications. Even though it is played with pretend money, and takes place on a pretend London the size of a carpet tile, watching his dearly beloved greedily trying to accrue the sort of property portfolio and wealth that would see them rubbing shoulders with elites, arms dealers and hedge fund managers is simply too much for him to bear. Finding out his wife has been skimming £50s each time she passes Go has been known to lead straight to the couch at Relate. Capitalism isn't a game, kids.

POKER

Like all dads, some part of Centrist Dad believes he might have it in him to be a master poker player. Sadly, the classic game of chance and guile relies on every instinct Centrist Dad has worked hard to suppress in himself. Greed, manipulation, gamesmanship and opportunism are all things he has stamped out in himself, and is trying to stamp out in his kids. Ironically this means that he has an excellent poker face because he just looks terribly anxious about the game the entire time and nobody has a clue whether he is holding a strong hand or not. Sadly, he does not have the instinct to take advantage of this superpower and is usually actively working to be the first person out so he can unclench his buttocks and take his ridiculous sunglasses off.

CHESS

Chess is *literally* a war game whose pieces symbolise everything that is unfair about how human society is structured. It's therefore no surprise that assigning higher value to a monarch than a mere sacrificial pawn, whilst trying to take prisoners from your opponent with absolutely no attempt to come to some sort of bilateral dialogue-based agreement first, is not Centrist Dad's favourite way to relax. The fact that this beastly endeavour takes place on a board that is *literally black and white* with not a single nuanced grey square is enough to cause our old friend a nosebleed. Hard no.

ANYTHING WITH DICE

Yahtzee, Ludo, Backgammon, Liar's Dice, Bunco, Midnight and Pig all have one thing in common. They are played by rolling dice. Asking Centrist Dad to roll dice is like asking him to get on a sledge at the top of a steep cliff. The very idea of voluntarily taking the risk of *mere chance* deciding his fate sounds absolutely insane to him. Don't even bother telling him that the wrong score could see him having to go backwards or his brain might snap and make a boinggggg sound.

Centrist-Dad-Approved Games

SUPERGLUE JENGA

A Jenga set rustling around in its box looks like a bitmapped anxiety dream to Centrist Dad. But the day he tackled that fear by carefully building a Jenga tower with the aid of a strong adhesive was the day he conquered that fear. Yes, it was entirely not the point of the game and now nobody else can play with it ever again *but at least he had a go.* Of course, he then did the same thing with his jigsaw of the *White Album* cover and his Lego Death Star as the family looked on sadly. Bless him. It may well be worth letting Centrist Dad try this approach just to see his little face concentrating without the fear of collapse in his eyes.

BOTTOMLESS MUSICAL CHAIRS

This version of the time-honoured children's party favourite is an excellent way to get Centrist Dad playing along without panicking about who is going to lose, or feeling threatened by the dwindling number of chairs that characterizes the game in its traditional form. To play

Bottomless Musical Chairs you simply add in a chair immediately for every chair removed to make sure that everybody has somewhere comfortable to sit with their dignity intact. Just let him enjoy it.

ARM SUPPORTING

Trust Centrist Dad to dream up a non-competitive version of arm wrestling where not only is nobody thrown to the floor by muscular superiority, but where nobody even goes *nngggghhhhh* and tries to win at all. In Arm Supporting both participants assume the starter grip of classic arm-wrestling and then just stay there providing each other with the basis of a mutually beneficial arrangement along the lines of a cantilevered roof.

SINGLE-COLOUR CONNECT FOUR

Everybody loves Connect Four, even Centrist Dad. It is one of the world's most simple and best loved games and can be enjoyed by anyone from about 18 months upwards. It's just that it would be slightly less problematic if the idea was for the participants to work together to achieve the result that ultimately they all want, which is a row of four plastic coin things in a straight line. So why not play Connect Four with both players using *only one* colour? Not only is it quicker and fairer, it might even be a small, relaxing step towards a better, more co-operative world.

Centrist Dad's Podcasts

Centrist Dad loves his podcasts. In fact, he can't even remember what he did before podcasts.* He'd be lost without them. Podcasts are Centrist Dadnip. Some of them are so essential that they're on the way to being articles of faith.

Take *The Rest is Politics.* This is Centrist Dad's happy place. Alastair 'Very Very' Campbell and Rory 'Very Good' Stewart, the Beatles of Centrist Dads, happily talk their way through the political landscape twice a week – *disagreeing agreeably,* as they say – without pinning their colours (pale shades of red and blue) to any particular mast. They're well informed, which means Centrist Dad can quote them to sound clever and, unlike 98 per cent of podcasters, they're not insane (although they are both bagpipers, which is something science will one day hopefully explain, along with

---

* He listened to 6 Music. He still does.

why anyone falls for cryptocurrency and who eats the toffee penny in the Quality Street tin).

They're also delightfully modest. Campbell is a former journalist who only ever achieved the humble position of being the Prime Minister's Official Spokesperson as part of his job as Downing Street Press Secretary (and later Director of Communications and Strategy), and before podcasting Stewart had an unremarkable career as MP for Penrith and The Border, Secretary of State for International Development, Minister of State for Prisons, Minister of State for Africa and Chair of the Defence Select Committee, and also ran to be Mayor of London, leader of the Conservative

Centrist Dad having that week's opinions downloaded to his mind.

Party and Prime Minister of the United Kingdom of Great Britain and Northern Ireland.

Neither of them is particularly influential (as their friends Tony Blair, Hillary Clinton and His Majesty the King have repeatedly pointed out to them) and it is this combination of humility and soft power that has made them so essential to Centrist Dad.

See also: the one that George Osborne and Ed Balls do, which you understandably can't remember the name of because it doesn't matter. It's **Political Currency**. And even though you've just read that, you've already forgotten it, and are already in denial that you ever read it anyway. Sorry, read what?

But Centrist Dad isn't just interested in politics. He's also keen on current affairs. Enter **The News Agents,** the podcast which doesn't just have its own Centrist Dad in the form of Jon Sopel, but also a Centrist Mum (Emily Maitlis) and a Centrist Son (Lewis Goodall). A whole Centrist Family for Centrist Dad to vibe along with. When Centrist Dad listens to *The News Agents,* he can fantasise that he lives on Centrist Avenue, and that these people are his next-door neighbours and best friends.

Then there are the also-rans: they're easy to spot because they look like the already-rans.

The Times does one that looks like *The News Agents.* The *Guardian* does one that looks like *The Sports Agents.* Channel Four does one called *The Political Fourcast* which looks like everything else and none of the above at the same time.

One lesser-known podcast which Centrist Dad is very fond of is ***Not Just Another Jeremy.*** It came about when ex-Labour councillor Jeremy Peopleman, presenter of *The Jeremy Podcast,* joined forces with former Conservative special adviser Jeremy Endbell, presenter of the podcast *Another Jeremy.* Together, they have built a show 'containing 200 per cent Jeremy and nothing else'.

Not Just Another Jeremy, or 'N-JAJ,' as its fans call it, drops twice a week, with occasional 'Jeremergency' episodes when something Jeremical happens – like when Endbell's dog, a rough-haired pointer called Bojo, had puppies.

The pair's success is attributed to their relaxed likeability, says their agent. Here's how a recent episode opened.

JP: Welcome to another *Not Just Another Jeremy*. I'm not just another Jeremy: I'm Jeremy Peopleman.

JE: And I'm Jeremy Endbell, not just another Jeremy.

JP: How's your week been, Jez?

JE: Well, you know ... my daughter passed her Grade Two piano.

JP: Result.

JE: Literally, yes.

JP: Literally a result.

JE: What else? I got a new back wheel on my bike.

JP: What was up with the old one?

JE: Rusty spoke nipples.

JP: (Laughs)

JE: It's no laughing matter.

JP: Sorry. I just wasn't expecting that combination of words.

JE: 'Rusty spoke nipples.'

JP: Sounds like a porn star name. Rusty Spokenipples.

JE: Have we done porn star names? We haven't, have we?

JP: ...what, the...

JE: ...first pet's name and the street you grew up on.

JP: Yeah, right.

JE: Is this Safe For Work, by the way?

JP: Depends on the names. Go on. We can always cut this bit.

JE: So mine would be ... Buzz Bodmin.

JP: 'Buzz Bodmin'? 'Buzz Bodmin'? Seriously?

JE: Yep. We had a black lab called Buzz – after Buzz Armstrong.

JP: Not Buzz Lightyear?

JE: Not in 1977, no.

JP: Fair enough –

JE: And I lived on Bodmin Road.

JP: 'Buzz Bodmin.' Sounds like a shared Devon workspace. You know the sort. Posh coffee machines in the reception area. Adverts for lunchtime yoga sessions on the notice board.

JE: You're basically describing this place.

JP: I am, basically, describing this place. Except this is in Islington.

JE: Anyway, what's yours?

JP: Er ... Smudge Bridge.

JE: Huh.

JP: It's not very ... arousing, is it?

JE: It's not very anything. It could be some boring bit of Wiltshire.

JP: Now now. Don't want to upset the Wiltshire crowd.

JE: Well, they won't get upset, because there's no such place.

JP: As Wiltshire?

JE: No. Smudge Bridge. If I said, I don't know, Chippenham could be some boring bit of Wiltshire, fair enough to be annoyed.

JP: Still, you are saying that Wiltshire has its boring bits, which is a bit...

JE: Everywhere's got its boring bits, though.

JP: Yeah, but you don't need to single them out.

JE: I'm not.

JP: But you are suggesting that there are single-out-able bits of Wiltshire that you think are boring.

JE: No I'm not. I'm just saying everywhere's got boring bits. I'm not having a go at Wiltshire. If anything, I'm having a go at everywhere.

JP: And is that ... better?

JE: Well...

JP: I mean, do you want to be having a go at literally *everywhere?*

JE: It's egalitarian.

Centrist Dad's Guide to Getting Around

Ideally, Centrist Dad would exist forever at the exact midpoint between A and B, but when he needs to get from one to the other, a **folding bicycle** is his vehicle of choice.

The problem with a normal bike is the two wheels aren't on speaking terms. In fact, they *barely know the other exists* – not a good look for a form of transport which is meant to save the world. Not that looking good is the point. The point is to put doing good before looking good. Because that looks good.

But with a folding bike, the two sides are forced to come together in a harmonious meeting of wheels. The only other vehicle in the house that does this is the Bugaboo, but Centrist Dad can't go to work on that. Although that hasn't stopped him from trying.

Ideally, Centrist Dad would not use the **rail network** until it is out of the grasping hands of the shareholding elite (although he would rather it was called 'railway reform' than 'renationalisation', which sounds a bit lefty), but he has found a compromise position: taking his folding bike on the train means he is *still a cyclist,* and not a rail user. In the same vein, he's worked out that if he skateboards down the aisle next time he's on an **EasyJet** to the south of France, he's skating, *not* flying.

This is a simple bit of mental gymnastics for the Centrist Dad. Justifying the **Audi,** on the other hand, requires a level of suppleness worthy of a contortionist in a bottle.

Two Centrist Dads with their helmets still on, just in case.

Of *course* he feels bad about having a car. That's why he only uses it for the kids' clubs, going to the dump and nipping out to Sainsbury's Local for Parmesan when the spaghetti's already on.

I mean, how else is he supposed to get all the presents to the in-laws' at Christmas? You can't do that on an **e-scooter.** (Although he did buy one, in case that in some way made up for the car – but then he read something in *The Week* about the batteries catching fire so now it lives in the shed with the surfboard, the homebrew and the remains of his drum kit.)

And, although he wouldn't admit this to anyone, he misses *Top Gear.* (And he definitely wouldn't admit that James May was always his favourite.) Those three may have appeared to be petrol-headed edgelords, but it was all an act. Underneath the swagger and racism and violence, they were Centrist Dads through and through. Look at them: Clarkson went on to be a farmer, all worried about the environment; Richard Hammond does classic car restoration now, preserving bits of motoring heritage like a kindly volunteer; and James May did his *Man Lab* thing where he defused bombs and broke out of prison but also built a coracle and made his own toilet paper, showing that Centrist Dad can indulge his gung-ho side as long as he balances it with eco-sensitivity.

Centrist Dad knows the clock is ticking on the Audi, though – but, with eco-sensitivity in mind, he's got his argument ready.

1. It would now be environmentally irresponsible to get rid of the Audi until absolutely necessary.

2. But when we do, the next car will be an EV.

3. Tell you what: Audi make some tasty-looking EVs.

Centrist Dad's Fashion Tips

Centrist Dad is a fashion icon. Of sorts. OK, so he's no David Bowie or Harry Styles, but he's got something even the trailblazing Bowie could only have dreamed of: a gilet. Centrist Dad is nothing without his gilet. It's his signature look. (Although that's a misleading term, given that a signature is supposed to be unique, and all Centrist Dads dress the same.)

The gilet represents the very middle of the middle ground of clothing. A jacket has a left and right sleeve – which, you would think, makes it balanced. But the problem is, it still has a left and a right 'wing'. Which means one of them has to come first. And trying to remember which sleeve came first last time so the other one can come first this time is enough to make Centrist Dad's head hot. The wily gilet saw the route through this problem: *no sleeves.* No left or right wing. Nothing but the centre of the garment. An end to sleeve-ism.

Centrist Dad wearing his invisibility cloak,
the gilet.

It's also designed for all the centrist temperatures. It can be worn when it's warm, because it hasn't got any sleeves, but also when it's cold, because it's padded. And, like Centrist Dad, it can't abide extremes: it's no use at all when it's freezing out, and it would look ludicrous being worn in a heatwave.

Wearing a gilet is the perfect way of Centrist Dad looking purposeful, even if everyone knows it, and he, is roundly useless. It's basically a misleading uniform. He might look like he's about to do something practical or physical or even just plain helpful, but he isn't. He's probably just going to Robert Dyas to stare in wonder at the many lightbulbs before buying a pack of batteries he doesn't really need.

But the about-to-do-something-ness the gilet confers to Centrist Dad gives him permanent poise, and the air of someone on the go. This man can do things. He is capable of great achievements.* Like walking the dog. Or editing the dishwasher. They say everyone has a novel in them – well, this man in his gilet has a *tax return* in him. Imagine.

---

* Terms and conditions apply.

Centrist Dad's Taste: An Introduction to Bland but Hot

Centrist Dad, of course, is capable of getting excited. Just because he doesn't commit to positions, it doesn't mean he's beyond emotion. It's just that what excites him has to have certain characteristics. He can't get worked up about anything too showy or too glamorous, anything with pizzazz or bling. He doesn't go in for fabulous or glitzy or sassy or gnarly or novel or thrilling or seductive: what he goes in for is simple: Bland but Hot.

Bland but Hot means Centrist Dad can never get too excited, which would destroy his centrist cred. Bland but Hot makes the exciting accept-able and the acceptable exciting. You could say Bland but Hot was Centrist Dad's jam, but there are no bland or hot jams, unless you count chilli jam, but that shouldn't be allowed to call itself a jam as it's obviously just an overpriced dip that's got ideas above its station.

Centrist Dad knows it when he sees it, but for those with a less (or more) refined palate, here are some good examples of the Bland but Hot things Centrist Dad gets excited by:

Susanna Reid

Chicken tikka masala

Camping in the south of France

Take That (except Gary Barlow)

The Ford Focus convertible

The patio heater section of the Screwfix catalogue

Mr Darcy

Nando's PERinaise

The ironing

Hand driers

Even-handed breakfast bombshell Susanna Reid
is the original centristfold.

Chicken tikka massala, the plain omelette
of the curry world.

Microwave porridge

David Beckham

The purple headboard light in a
Premier Inn room

Bodyboarding

A Greggs Steak Bake

Mountain Warehouse gilets

Daphne from Scooby-Doo

Buffaloes

Basingstoke during a heatwave

Staining the shed

Ovaltine

The changing rooms at David Lloyd

A mild Cheddar fondue

Strictly Come Dancing

Hammocks

Camomile tea

Saxophone solos

Disposable barbecues

Electric blankets

Hovercraft

Any Centrist Dad reading this may now need to go and have a brief lie-down.

How Did We Get Here?

There was a time when 'centrist dad' was just a casual insult, like 'blithering faffcock' or 'Noel Edmonds', but now Centrist Dad is in charge.

Centrist Dads dominate our political, cultural, economic and sporting circles. They're at the highest levels of government. They run FTSE 100 companies. They sell out 20,000-seater venues. They edit newspapers. They present TV and radio shows. And podcasts. So many podcasts. And, most importantly, they piss Richard Littlejohn off something rotten.

So how did we get here? There are several theories.

One is that having a political class full of eccentrics, caricatures, weirdos and figures of fun at a time of absolute crisis taught us all a valuable lesson: you don't want the pilot of the plane you're in to be an eccentric, a caricature, a weirdo or a figure of fun, in case there's an absolute crisis – because no amount of eccentricity or fun can help you out of a plane crash.

Another is that being dull and reasonable has now become fashionable – a theory which would also explain the popularity of Ed Sheeran, oat milk and the Billy bookcase.

A third is that the middle-aged men who somehow always end up controlling everything have an unresolved yearning for their younger selves and the happier world they lived in, which for the present generation of middle-aged men was the late 90s: the Centrist Dad of today is basically the reborn Blairite, returning us to a world in which it is somehow always 1997.

Homo Centrus regards himself as the next stage in the evolution of humankind.

And there are more outlandish theories. Is Centrist Dad a construct promoted by Russian bot farms? Is Centrist Dad a communist/fascist in disguise? Is Centrist Dad a marketing opportunity turned demographic stereotype, like Mondeo Man?

Perhaps the most intriguing theory is one advanced by a self-aware Centrist Dad, investigating the subject from the inside: Jon Ronson. Here is an excerpt from his new podcast series (what else?), *The Pesto Parallax*.

Jon Ronson's *The Pesto Parallax*

INTRODUCTION

Hello. I'm Jon Ronson. An A-League Centrist Dad who talks in stops. And starts. Like this. And this.

Welcome to *The Pesto Parallax*, my new podcast series that wasn't quite convincing enough to become a book. Or a film. In it, I make the argument that the journey of Centrist Dadism in British Society has remarkable similarities to the journey of pesto. Over eight episodes, or maybe more if it goes well, I will ponder the question of whether pesto is just a harmless, time-saving, child-friendly stir-through pasta sauce. Or if our entire social and political spectrum has been recalibrated by the slow integration of a store-cupboard staple, that none of us had ever heard of.

Until one day, something happened.

NESSUN DORMANT

On 7 August 1990, as the England football team were struggling to find a winning goal in the World Cup semi-final in the Italian city of Turin, tens of millions of British men were united by only two things: Carling Black Label and furiously wanting to beat their most bitter enemy. Germany. Who they then referred to universally as the Krauts or the Bosch – a hangover from the nicknames Allied soldiers had given the Nazis during the Second World War. Which was already ages ago.

But then, something happened.

Paul Gascoigne, a talented goofball from Newcastle who played in midfield, flew into a bad tackle and was booked, meaning he would definitely miss the final even if England won, which they didn't, because they never do. Gascoigne – or Gazza, as he was known – burst into tears on the pitch, like a five-year-old who had been told to go to bed while his big brother was

Paul Gascoigne wiping away the first ever
traces of male vulnerability.

allowed to stay up and watch *Nightmare on Elm Street*. Gazza was the first British man to cry on TV. Ever.

This outburst of raw human emotion played out in front of over 35 million British men who ordinarily tried to suppress feeling anything other than lager-fuelled anger.

But then, something happened.

Paul's teammate, England's top scorer Gary Lineker, wiggled his boyish eyes towards the team's bench, throwing a sort of non-committal grimace that seemed to say, 'I'm a bit worried about Paul.' Lineker was the first British man to admit to worrying about a Paul ever. In that moment, the raw materials of British male compassion were born.

But then, something happened.

Because when clips of this new modern crying were replayed, over and over, accompanied by the sound of Luciano Pavarotti singing Puccini's 'Nessun Dorma', a significant percentage of British men found themselves wanting to hold on to this new feeling of cautiously acknowledging emotions, at the same time as liking something that sounded a bit foreign. And cultured. It was, to put it mildly, confusing.

But then, something happened.

Just one day after the game, in a supermarket in Islington, North London, a jar of previously unheard-of pasta sauce called *pesto* was plucked from a shelf and put into a basket by a hungover English man humming 'Nessun Dorma' to himself. Because he didn't know any of the words. Which were in Italian and too slow to understand anyway.

The first steps towards Centrist Dad had been taken.

But in which direction would they head?

In those early days pesto and Centrist Dad each had only one flavour: classic basil and John Major, who was about to become probably the least disagreeable Prime Minister Britain had ever seen.

MAJOR CHANGES

Within four hours of John Major becoming Prime Minister everyone was bored shitless of him. Even though nothing he was saying was anywhere near as bad as nearly everything that has happened since. In an instant, sensible, decisive and moderate men all over Britain realised that just because they were boring, didn't mean they had to eat peas every single night for the rest of their lives.

And it was into this vacuum that pesto's popularity began to rise. Prototype Centrist Dads began to see pesto as a logical, convenient alternative to other more fiddly main ingredients, like pork chops, and sauté potatoes. Why go through the rigmarole of browning mince and onions for an amateurish bolognese when he could just stir a few teaspoons of an exotic new paste through his spaghetti or penne, straight out of a jar that even his effete, white-collar wrists could open? It made early Centrist Dad feel sophisticated in ways that mince could never *dream* of.

The continental miracle-in-a-jar that changed everything.

But then, something happened.

As the 90s advanced, 'New Lads' like Neil Morrissey and David Baddiel arrived on the scene, ushered in by *Loaded* magazine and its brazen glorification of nipples, binge-drinking and kebabs. Men who actually *did* know better, because they weren't immature little knuckle-draggers, felt left behind. Uncool and unseen. And with their wild days of debauchery and hot sex behind them, they turned away from lad culture, slipped into their fleeces and became dads. Centrist Dads.

By 1997, 89 per cent of knackered parents were serving pesto and pasta to their children up to six times per week and could no longer be arsed making anything else – because the kids were eating it, no questions asked, often with their fists. And out of cereal bowls.

But then, something happened.

Tony Blair became Prime Minister, with his snake-oil rebranding of a Labour Party that was now based in Islington instead of where there are any working-class people at all. Instead of Neil Kinnock and Roy Hattersley, they now had figures like Alastair Campbell, Jonathan Ross, Noel Gallagher and Mr Blobby as trendy new members. Centrist Dad began to feel that he might be in the cool club again.

Tony Blair was photographed holding an electric guitar on purpose, in a way that made him look like an

accountant who had jumped on stage at the Shadows'
Christmas party. And in that exact moment, as culture
was taking Centrist Dad towards the bright new lights
of hope, a new pesto flavour was introduced: red pesto.
Just as is the case with red Thai curry, nobody knows or
cares why it's red. Or why it's not green. All that matters
is that now Centrist Dad had *a choice of pestos.**

The experiment worked. And, by the turn of the millen-
nium, both colours of pesto and Tony Blair's New Labour
project were dominant forces in British culture. Free
market capitalism went bat-shit crazy and before long
it felt like there were new pesto flavours appearing on
supermarket shelves every week. Wild mushroom pesto.
Sun dried tomato pesto, which was red for an *identifiable*
reason (tomatoes). Charred aubergine and garlic pesto.
And even coriander and chilli pesto, even though that
sounds horrible on pasta. The genie was out of the jar.
This was becoming a full-blown foodie frenzy. A free-for-
all. A flavour-off . . . which became known as *The Pesto
Parallax.* (Which is the name of my new podcast.)

The most powerful families in Britain were no longer
the Krays, the Richardsons or the Windsors. They were
the proudly Italian Saclà and Dolmio families, the latter
subsequently revealing themselves to be unnerving

---

* Even Centrist Dad Jon Ronson can't bring himself to
say 'pesti'.

felt puppets in a TV ad campaign. But the public didn't care. They were glamorous and continental. And, far from being Mafioso style criminals making their money through bullion robberies, protection rackets or class-A drugs, the Saclà and Dolmio clans were becoming billionaires by putting simple ingredients in a blender and selling them to an increasing audience of timepoor men, who started to realise that they could cook a trendy Italian dish without having to do anything at all.

But then, something happened.

The image of Centrist Dad began to change. Bill Clinton was filmed in the Oval Office lying out of his Arkansas arsehole about his affair with young White House intern Monica Lewinsky. Meanwhile, in the UK, Centrist Dads were becoming disillusioned with the pesto in their fridges, as they started to realise that if they left it for more than two weeks, it grew a layer of green fur. Making it inedible.

Centrist Dad started to doubt himself, and chicken Kyivs and oven-ready lasagnes began to out-perform pesto for the first time in years. Clinton's out of control presidential penis had blown the world's trust in white, male, middle-aged, skilled mediators out of the water. Centrist Dad was dead in the water. Having fallen back into the water after having been blown out of it upwards.

But then, something happened.

OLIVER'S ARMY

Jamie Oliver arrived on Britain's TVs and began acting like he had invented the whole of cooking. Centrist Dad quickly fell in love with Oliver and soon he was an underserving, raffish demi-god. The wanky pesto flavour floodgates crashed wide open and have never closed since. Now, in pubs and snooker halls throughout the land, self-identified blokes shamelessly began talking competitively about stirring pulsed cauliflower and lemon rind or beetroot and radicchio through hand-rolled pasta made in little metal machines that they had put on their John Lewis wedding lists. These were the same men who had once talked about Linda Lusardi or Frank Bruno out of the side of their mouths, before fighting each other while still holding a bag of chips.

People started wearing trainers with suits. Rock stars became artisan cheese makers. At one point, Blur's Alex James threatened to sue Chris Martin for plagiarising one of his goat's cheese recipes in a Coldplay song about sustainable farming.

But then, something happened.

Suddenly the rapid spread of decadent, middle-class tastes that respected other cultures began to make some British people (who hated foreign things, except curry and Chinese, which they had five times a week) crave a new figurehead. One that didn't make them feel stupid and small-minded, even though that is exactly what they were. It was into this vacuum that Nick Griffin, the portly, glass-eyed leader of the British Nationalist Party, stepped, full of subtle new ideas like pretending not to be racist whilst still actively seeking to deport anyone who wasn't white. As anti-European sentiment began to grow, Griffin took to making traditional British Fayre on his YouTube channel, Nick Griffin's Paranoid Racist Dinners (YouTube was new and exciting then). Horrified by pesto's omnipresence, Griffin tried to make an English version with cabbage, mild Cheddar, Smith's plain crisps and Bombardier beer. He was quickly copied by a slew of patriotic idiots. Who found out it was nothing like pesto. And it tasted like when sick comes out.

It was now 2009 and Centrist Dad didn't know which pesto was safe for him to be seen tossing on his pasta anymore. Pesto had lost its glossy sheen. It was seen as the dinner of the weak and lazy. It was briefly redeemed by 'nduja pesto, which was made of sausages and tasted of fire, but it felt like the moment had passed. Meanwhile in the public eye, Centrist Dad was nowhere to be seen. Everyone had realised that Tony Blair was a grinning, opportunist, cowardly grifter who would punch himself off a cliff if America told him to. He wasn't even Prime Minister anymore.

Increasingly extreme figures started to attract support, as social media handed everyone their own individual megaphone that came straight from their arseholes. Russell Brand warned everyone off voting and then started a cult to hide whatever it is he really is. Jeremy Corbyn glued his lips together on International Holocaust Day. Donald Trump grinned after being adjudicated a rapist. And Boris Johnson stayed on holiday longer than it took for a pandemic to shut a whole country down. Everywhere was angry. Nothing was working. And pesto began to represent a lack of self-care and imagination synonymous with major depressive disorder.

But then, something happened.

The culture wars were beginning to stir, and they began to be reflected in an insanely paranoid new subset of pestos that catered for every hue of identity politics. The supermarket shelves were by now a confusing mosaic of light pesto, gluten-free pesto, Fairtrade pesto, reduced fat pesto, vegan pesto, freegan pesto, alt-right pesto, pesto with added Sudocrem, pesto with gender-neutral 3D-printed cheese, pumpkin spiced oat latte pesto – and an invisible pesto developed by the CIA that didn't sell because nobody believed it was there.

It was no wonder the newly emboldened Centrist Dads that had taken over the world of podcasting longed to return to the simplicity of the original pesto revolution sparked by Paul Gascoigne crying through his big red football face all those years ago...

This snippet of *The Pesto Parallax* is only the beginning of the story that I have somehow concocted using basic narrative structure techniques, combined with my soft, slightly unusual voice. That stops. And starts. Like this. And this.

Come and listen to the whole series. And I will tell you all about the pestorati, a lost tribe of Centrist Dads who now live in the Calabrian countryside foraging their own basil while gently cupping each other's balls. Learn about what happened to the Middlesborough Mince Mountain that grew to the size of Ben Nevis when nobody could be arsed making bolognese anymore. And let me tell you how Jeff Bezos nearly spunked his whole fortune on turning Mars into the world's first off-world Big Pesto farm, before realising that the world had already altered its point of view and was now facing toward a new player in the be-jarred store-cupboard trendy-verse. Behold. Kimchi. Which I will probably attempt to turn into a follow-up podcast series straight after this.

After all, what is a parallax, if it isn't conclusive proof that if you view things from an acute enough angle, nobody checks whether what you are saying is an absolute load of pecorino. Or Parmesan. Or piffle.

Centrist Dad's Enemies

Centrist Dad, of course, has his opponents – and, unhelpfully for him, they come from both sides. Right-wingers disagree with left-wingers, and left-wingers disagree with right-wingers; but *both right and left* disagree with the centre, because from where they're standing, the centre is also to the right, or left, of them.

In truth, Centrist Dad *should* be politically homeless, because he's always to the left of the right and to the right of the left. Centrism can mean borrowing opinions from both sides – but it can also mean having no opinion at all. So poor Centrist Dad can be criticised for *opinions which he doesn't have.*

This is Centrist Dad's problem. Because he agrees with some of the right and some of the left, he annoys both of them because it means he *disagrees with some of the right and some of the left.* And disagreement trumps agreement in politics, because shouting is louder than nodding.

In other words: *Centrist Dad is a sitting target.* Which is why he needs to *know his enemies*.

THE RIGHT. These are the people who get most annoyed by Centrist Dad. They think he's mimsy, feckless, docile, smug, twatty and too left-wing.

THE LEFT. These are also the people who get most annoyed by Centrist Dad. They also think he's mimsy, feckless, docile, smug, twatty – but too right-wing.

THE LADS. They've got no time for fucking cyclists.

THE ANARCHO-CENTRISTS. A maverick bunch. They believe in revolutionary centrism, with agreeability, not importance or need, as the chief basis for social status in their frighteningly mild (or is it mildly frightening?) utopia.

THE NEO-CENTRISTS. These are the people who argue for a new centre. It's not clear (even to them) whether they have a point.

HIS MUM. She's bound to be an old socialist/ capitalist/nationalist of some sort, or he wouldn't have rebelled himself into a centrist position in the first place. But, she's his mum, and he can't shout at her, which is how he calmly arrived at his no-fuss, say-as-little-as-possible centrist position in the first place. And he loves her. But she is – make no mistake – part of the problem. And she thinks *he's* part of the problem.

THE PRESS. Usually, they start circling the victim when they smell blood. In Centrist Dad's case, the beast was awoken by the smell of his moisturiser.

SOCIAL MEDIA. Although, to be fair, social media hates everybody and loves hate. No-one can win.

BREXIT. Obviously. It was a deranged binary. He'd rather not talk about it.

HIS KIDS (POTENTIALLY). As they grow up and develop their own politics, they're likely to cleave away from their dad's opinions. This is how seemingly reasonable people end up with children who join Just Stop Oil or whatever Nigel Farage's army of gobshites is called this week.

SUPERMARKET TROLLEYS. Always dragging him this way and that. Centrist Dad wants to go forward, not be forced left or right. The houmous is straight over there, and doesn't need to be reached via the dog food and the tampons.

Nobody tells Centrist Dad which way to go.

ROUNDABOUTS. They force him to go left. (Or right, if abroad.) Unspeakable. The only acceptable roundabout is that one in Swindon which goes in *both* directions.

HUNGRY AND/OR TIRED TODDLERS. Toddlers are delightful, but not when they're crying or yelling about basic human needs. And if being on the end of this racket wasn't bad enough, these micro-aggressors cannot be reasoned with, yet still require Centrist Dad to be reasonable. His basic nightmare.

PUNK ROCK. Grown adults doing what hungry and/or tired toddlers do, but via the medium of snarling and guitars.

WILD HORSES. Probably.

JUNK MAIL. How dare an unsolicited mail-drop make so many assumptions about him? His gutters are fine, thank you, and he doesn't like Domino's.

WIND. More pressure to go in a given direction.

SLOPES. Same.

ACTIVISTS. Why do people feel the need to gather and shout? You won't find Centrist Dad out there shouting at people to be more reasonable. That doesn't seem reasonable.

DECISION TREES. Nightmare.

WASPS. Centrist Dad isn't alone here. Wasps are everyone's enemy. Stripy little shits.

Centrist Dad's Guide to Food Shopping

Food shopping for Centrist Dad is a minefield. Where to go? What else to buy? Whether to have a loyalty card? Whether to admit to having a loyalty card? Who to admit that to? How to hide it from the others?

Some food shops are refreshingly unjudgeable, and can be comfortably visited by anyone. Others are the shopping equivalent of a voting poster in a porch window, and must be avoided for fear of humiliation.

Let's start with the Big Ones.

Centrist Dad is going to find himself completely at home in **Sainsbury's** and **Tesco**. These are apolitical spaces. Even the foodstuffs are apolitical here. Centrist Dad could walk out of either supermarket with a Charlie Bigham's pie or a packet of Midland Snacks pork scratchings and he would not be making any sort of statement, because everything is beyond judgement in Sainsbury's and Tesco. These are *safe spaces* for Centrist Dad, and he can buy whatever he likes here.

(Plus, they both sell quite good pants, which is helpful, because no-one can decide how they feel about **M&S** these days, except that it's still very much Mum territory for some reason. Probably something to do with bras.)

But if Centrist Dad buys a Charlie Bigham's pie at **Waitrose**, or a packet of Midland Snacks pork scratchings at **Asda**, he is making a political purchase. He may as well put his pie in the boot of his Rolls-Royce and his scratchings in the footwell of his stock car. Context is everything.

In short, unless it's a secret mission, or he goes shopping in disguise,* Centrist Dad is better off avoiding the following supermarkets: Morrison's, Asda, Waitrose, Iceland, Whole Foods, Aldi, Planet Organic and Booths.

If Centrist Dad wants everyone to *know* he's a centrist, then he should make a beeline for the **Co-Op**. The Co-Op is the James O'Brien of supermarkets: utterly reasonable, ever so slightly untidy, and absolutely everywhere. Shopping there is making a statement, but a very mild, very

---

* Or goes shopping *ironically*, which is hard (but not impossible) to do.

centrist statement. Centrist Dad is not given to showing off his centrism, but if he wants to, co-opting the Co-Op is one good way. (And if he really wants to up the performative centrism, he should be seen carrying reusable bags from two other, different supermarkets at different ends of the shopping spectrum.)

The dark horse of centrist food shopping is **Lidl**. The jury's out on where it sits on the political spectrum, because it's German, and German politics are dominated by confusing coalitions that make no sense to anyone else.

For instance, the German government at the time of writing is made up of the social democrats, the greens and the liberals – except that the liberals or Thatcherites who used to be left-wing, and are socially liberal, are also being infiltrated by anti-woke American libertarians. Completely incomprehensible.

Similarly, Lidl is a confusing coalition of products. It sells fantastically cheap toilet paper and excellent knock-off craft beer for a fraction of the cost of the real thing, but also about 400 different cured meats of the type you'd get in a restaurant where it's £28 for a bowl of fucking risotto. Plus, in the central aisle (the Middle of Lidl) you can buy (checks notes) power tools and Oriental Lilies (this week). It's no wonder no-one can pin it down.

Independent shops require careful consideration. Of course, Centrist Dad wants to support the independent sector — but he must do so at no cost to his reputation. So when sizing up an independent, look for signs. Avoid anywhere with plastic bowls of assorted fruit and veg outside for sale at fixed prices. Avoid anywhere with an A-board on the pavement that mentions either barbecues or bubbles. Avoid any cheese shop where the person behind the counter looks like they want to be noticed by a modelling agency. Avoid anything with a poster for a demonstration in the window. And avoid any shop that sells *just one foodstuff* for which there shouldn't be a shop: fudge, for instance, or mustard.*

How Centrist is Your Food?

Some foods skew fairly obviously left or right. **Foie gras**, for instance, is clearly right-wing: it's got a French name and one of its ingredients is torture. It's so right-wing, in fact, that some territories have made it the world's first illegal pâté.

---

* There is a mustard *boutique* in London's Piccadilly Arcade. It must be stopped.

Anything you could conceivably **keep as a pet** is also a right-wing foodstuff, with the exception of goats, because you can't make a Greek salad without them. **Houmous** is almost as left-wing as it gets, except that it is outflanked by **kale**, the Jeremy Corbyn of brassicas.

Anything which was **shot** is right-wing, and anything which is a **non-dairy** version of a dairy product is left-wing. The one exception to this is margarine, because old people use it.

Beware especially of foods that are trying far too hard to place themselves on the edges of the political spectrum, like Billy Bragg's range of salad dressings and the AfD's Hitler Shapes in Tomato Sauce.

Removing an avocado stone is the single most dangerous moment in Centrist Dad's week.

Some foods, however, change politically depending on their context.

Centring Your Meal

Take the **Full English Breakfast**. A reasonable gut reaction (no pun intended) would be to assume that it's right-wing, meaning Centrist Dad would have to rule it out. But times have changed, and many a Full English is now comfortably centrist, thanks to some careful tweaking.

The basics of a Full English are bacon, egg, sausage, tea and toast. So far, so right-wing. But a good fancy sausage, full of herbs, pulls the basics towards Centrist Dad's sweet spot, and wholemeal bread does a lot of heavy lifting (and virtue-signalling). Just a few more considerations and this is a plate of centrist heaven.

Baked beans (which fundamentally have no place on a Full English, being American and ruinous, but anyway) come in a range of political colours. The approved centrist way to serve them is in a ramekin. But beware: if they're home-made baked beans, things are drifting to the left. Black pudding used to be roundly right-wing, but some of it is now so artisanal that it's almost impossible to gauge (although it is aggressively non-vegan).

The sprig of parsley in this breakfast will help to calm Centrist Dad down when he sees the beans.

Hash browns: left-wing. Mushrooms: left-wing. Burford Brown eggs: just right of centre. Eggs from the breakfast maker's own hens: *very* right-wing. Spinach: where do you think this is? The House of Lords?*

Centrist Dad's ideal Full English, then, is a tricky business. And, since everything about its preparation is largely out of his hands, may be a

---

* Presentation can be misleading: if a Full English Breakfast is served on a shovel, this does not mean that a working class person got it out of a kiln.

risk too far. Safer to stick to porridge. Centrist Dad knows where he is with porridge: back in the land of the Bland but Hot.

Fish and chips present a similar political conundrum. Long the country's national dish, they arrived in Britain thanks to Jewish immigrants from southern Europe – making them solidly left-wing and the workers' food. But again, they're sort of Brexit-y now. The solution is to serve the chips in a stupid little wire basket, and suddenly everything's resolutely centrist. Similarly, mushy peas are left-wing, but add mint and they're centrist.

Centrist Dad will, of course, fret about what sort of fish is inside that batter, because he's read more contradictory press stories about which fish are sustainable than he has about whether red wine is good for you, bad for you, or just red wine for you. He's only one step away from downloading the Marine Stewardship Council app, so he can get alerts on what he's allowed to eat.

He knows there are a couple of fish which are always mentioned, so they must be sustainable: coley and pollock. But he doesn't know what either of them is like, or even what either of them looks like. Are they as nice as cod and haddock? They sound like they might even be the new words for cod and haddock – like when Bombay suddenly became Mumbai.*

As to the sides, pickled onions are a hard no, unless they're ironic. Tartare sauce is acceptable, but home-made is better. And although everyone wants there to be sliced white bread with their fish and chips – well, bad luck, Centrist Dad. Being seen with sliced white bread? You might as well walk around in a Union Jack vest.

Indeed, **bread** is a headache for Centrist Dad in general. White is out, but all the new breads (seeded sourdough, potato bread, semolina bread, pide, flatkaka, anything gluten-free and anything namechecking 'ancient grains') are a bit hoity-toity. Wholemeal or wholegrain is the safe space of the bread universe.

Pizza is a moveable feast – both literally and politically. A McCain cheese and tomato one done under the grill is a bit too flat-roofed pub for Centrist Dad. (See also: the Domino's Meateor.) Anything branded by Pizza Express, on the other hand: perfect. No-one can judge Centrist Dad for that. Pizza Express is the

---

* One of these days, Centrist Dad will find out that pollock is what's in a McDonald's Filet-O-Fish and for a moment, there'll be no turning back. Then he'll start to worry that McDonald's isn't centrist, and his fish fears will start all over again. Sometimes, he can't win.

Volkswagen Golf of food brands. Don't go too far, though. An entirely-home-made-from-scratch-including-the-dough Margherita cooked in the garden in one of those Ooni pizza ovens under a 'Casa Di Papa' sign from the garden centre is, if anything, *too centrist*. There's only so much centrism a family can take. Shudder.

Avoiding Edible Cultural Appropriation

Centrist Dad is always sensitive to cultural appropriation, and sometimes it's hard to find the right compromise with food. The word 'pizza', for instance, means 'pie' in Italian, and a pizza is not a pie in any sense at all. But if Centrist Dad is feeling particularly sensitive about not wanting to pass off as Italian, he can refer to it as an Italian two-minute dough circle. He might sound mad saying this, but at least he won't sound racist.

Other substitute food names:

Burrito: *swaddled Mexican-style meat and friends*

Dal: *Indian-inspired lentil surprise*

Hot Dog: *American open-top sausage roll*

Tagine: *North African casserole in a ceramic hat*

Jerk Chicken: *colonial chicken apology*

Bánh Mì: *Vietnamese-adjacent everything sandwich*

Coq au vin: *bird dans le booze*

Baba ganoush: *crushed aubergine ruins*

Katsu curry: *they do this at Wagamama*

In the Kitchen

What's in Centrist Dad's kitchen cupboards will be judged by others, so he needs to play his pots and pans game carefully. Because of course he wants a nice solid **Le Creuset** pan he can do every other meal in. But it's Le Creuset, the Hunter's wellies of the casserole world. How's Centrist Dad going to pull that off?

The answer is offsetting.

Centrist Dad can have his Le Creuset, as long as he offsets it with a Breville Sandwich Maker he uses at least once a year, however badly the molten cheese burns his mouth. And there are plenty more offsets he can make in the kitchen. He can own a nutribullet as long as he's got four tins of marrowfat peas in the cupboard at all times. He can own a cocktail shaker as long as he's got a jelly mould. He can even have a wine fridge – but only if it's half-filled with Diet Coke. And speaking of wine…

How Centrist is Your Drink?

What Centrist Dad drinks also takes a bit of thought.

Obviously, he likes **craft beer**. And not just half-craft brands like Brewdog and Beavertown. He goes in for the beers with silly names like 'Purple Monkey Dishwasher', 'The Window's Accusing the Door of Abusing the Wall', and 'Set Breakfast #1 (No Substitutions)'.

But the ones he *talks about* are the alcohol-free ones, because these are both fashionable and virtuous, so he can talk about *how great they taste* and *how you'd never know they were alcohol-free,* neither of which is true, because they taste alcohol-free, which is how you know they're alcohol-free.

Bubbles present Centrist Dad with a dilemma. He doesn't want to be accused of being a *Champagne socialist,* although that term is now nearly as old as he is. (Conversely, he doesn't want to be whatever the opposite is. A *Carlsberg capitalist,* perhaps?) Centrist Dad could easily get tripped up showing compassion for the working classes at a middle-class dinner party where nobody earns less than £120,000 when someone more right-wing scoffs at him – so he never goes above prosecco. A glass of prosecco is the safe, class-free fizz.

Wine as a whole is automatically centrist, especially rosé, a wine that can't decide if it's red or white so sticks to the comfortable centre. **Spirits**, on the other hand, are a nightmare. Who can gauge the politics of a twelve-year old single malt? It could be anything. It could be an authoritarian fascist or a liberal communitarian. One thing's for sure: it's definitely not centrist. See also: brandy, sherry, rum, gin and port. (Although port's probably dyed-in-the-wool Tory.)

Vodka is, fortunately, classless, but there are so many upstart fancy-pants mixers these days (made with botanicals, whatever they are: posh compost?) that it's almost impossible not to look a bit of a twanny ordering one.

Centrist Dad and his Pressure Washer

Centrist Dad has a unique relationship with his pressure washer. The two of them are very close. It's nothing to be worried about – he's not having an affair with it. Although he is impressed by and fascinated with it, like he sometimes is with a new colleague or someone who works behind the bar at the holiday resort. The difference here is that his other half doesn't shoot him shitty looks when he's with his pressure washer: instead, they're looks of serious concern.

Like the Christmas decorations, the pressure washer only comes out once a year. But when it does, on Pressure-Washing Day (observance varies, but it's usually sometime in late spring), Centrist Dad absolutely goes to town with it. Because pressure-washing is like smoking crack, and it doesn't take long before Centrist Dad is in the zone and way down a P-hole.

The Marilyn Monroe of Centrist Dad's shed.

He starts with the patio. Of course he does. This takes some time, and is sensible and justified. Centrist Dad likes being sensible and justified, and if he spends enough time on the patio, it balances out everything that follows.

Next up come the gutters. This is also sensible and justified, but less sensible because he pressure-washes all the muck out of the gutters and onto the newly cleaned patio. So he then has to chase all the junk off the newly cleaned patio into the gulleys and drains. And then it's the drains' turn to be pressure-washed. This is all thought out and planned in advance, because that deliberate mistake with the gutter muck is a bit of theatre that says: *Centrist Dad isn't infallible; he can get things wrong, you know.* And it buys him the opportunity to make further, sometimes deliberate, mistakes.

Next up is the underneath of the Flymo. All that grass has been stuck there for a year now, and Centrist Dad wants rid of the dead green so he can revel in the bright orange again. Then, thinking laterally, he gets the garden broom and pressure-washes all the grass out of that. *And if that brush can be pressure-washed*, thinks Centrist Dad, *then there are … other brushes that can too.*

This is where it begins.

Centrist Dad sends the kids to bring the toilet brushes out into the garden. And, being careful to fire the water into a hedge or the compost, zaps all the difficult stuff out of them. Centrist Dad is now a warrior. He is vanquishing his tagnut enemies. He is destroying a year's worth of scrub castaways. HE IS LEGEND.

He is also, quite frankly, losing it.

He may now try to pressure-wash next door's overhanging tree back into their garden. This will not work.* Nor will trying to pressure-

---

* And may cause the neighbours to lose it.

wash fox shit off the dog.* But remember: *Centrist Dad isn't infallible; he can get things wrong, you know.*

By the time Centrist Dad is trying to pressure-wash pigeons off the extension roof, he is in full combat mode, and requires an intervention in the form of unplugging the pressure washer. He will immediately return to his reasonable self, and will probably calmly take the pressure washer out to the front garden and make a start on the path. He should get into no trouble here: there are fewer targets out on the street, because Centrist Dad can't be seen to be a pressure-warrior in public. It would ruin his reputation locally. And no neighbourhood ever needs a new weirdo. This should be enough to stop him taking fire at a cat, but if he's had a lot of coffee that day, keep an eye on him. There are also certain lines that must absolutely never be crossed.

---

* And *will* cause the dog to lose it.

Don't let Centrist Dad use the pressure washer for...

- Getting spinach out from between his teeth
- Destroying wasps' nests
- Joining in with the kids' Super Soaker battle
- Removing stubborn earwax
- Getting the scratches off CDs
- Giving the tomato plants a 'quick once over' (unless you want passata)
- Trying to get rid of his moobs

Gary Lineker:
A Warning from History

Sometimes a political figure comes along who completely reshapes what we understand about society and life itself, changing the course of human history forever in the process. Gary Lineker – when he goes on Twitter – is such a man.

Since winning the Golden Boot in the 1986 World Cup in Mexico with a series of masterful tap-ins from four yards out, Gary had been grinning and gently rolling his eyes at us, and sometimes with us, in a manner that is entirely consistent with the Centrist Dad character profile. For over 30 years there was nobody in the United Kingdom that would have been more equally welcome at your mother's dinner table and your brother-in-law's stag do at the go-karting. He was the human equivalent of those Styrofoam fillers they put in boxes that look like Wotsits before the flavour is put on. His sharp

Centrist Dad Gary Lineker shamelessly pulls
his tie slightly to the left.

but unflashy shirts and gently tanned skin gave lesser men an example of self-care, vitality and self-assuredness to look up to as they sank into the hollows of their dank leatherette armchairs, their replica football shirts dusted with snack crumbs, dented cans of supermarket lager lying around their coffee tables like the glorious dead.

And yet, despite his towering superiority, there was not a hint of malice towards the man from anyone, anywhere. Why? Because he was Gary from Leicester. *The* Centrist Dad hero. The top-scoring England golden boy who never even received a yellow card in his entire playing career. The goofily handsome lad whose dancing eyes had shown the whole world he had Paul Gascoigne's back that dreadful night in 1990.

By the time he arrived on our screens as a presenter, TV Gary Lineker 1.0 (let's call him) was perfectly formed and ready to be received warmly. He looked as clean as a humanoid and when he spoke, he judged nothing and nobody, instead simply stating the facts and posing a few gently cheeky questions which were carefully tempered by a disarming shrug of his beautiful shoulders.

In some ways he was both ubiquitous and invisible at the same time, cushioned as he was by highlights packages of beautiful goals, debates about dodgy refereeing decisions, and – lest we forget – Mark Lawrenson. These were the things Britain could project its dreams and its anger onto with unthinking moral impunity, often while trying not to actively nod off. What a position from which to grow into a nation's hearts. Lineker's easy, non-offensive charm was the secret recipe that secured him a mainstream BBC career that came to straddle several decades.

Over time his hair may have started slowly greying, but his slim frame maintained its graceful stature, and Britain as a nation had no idea what he thought about anything beyond ballsed-up England penalty shoot-outs and the lack of midfield shape in several post-Ferguson Manchester United teams. And that was the way Britain liked it.

So skilled was Lineker's ability to offend absolutely no-one that even becoming the world's most over-remunerated crisp mascot and having human gristle-mound Wayne Lineker as a brother left his image without so much as a hairline scratch.

And then he joined Twitter.

As for so many of us, having access to a loud-hailer you can use from the toilet or during a meal with someone who is no longer interesting to you began to be a source of sweet, sweet nectar for Gary. No longer constrained by an autocue laden with smug asides that a passive-aggressive writer had decided sounded like him, Gary had something he'd never had before, because we didn't need him to have it. A voice.

And when you have 8.8 million followers reacting to your every utterance, a voice can become like one of those dragons out of *Game of Thrones:* difficult to control, imbued with a sense of power and annoyingly fucking noisy. (Though, to be fair, he has never set a bunch of peasants on fire at the command of a nineteen-year-old queen.)

Post-joining Twitter, it slowly became clear that, far from living on a special chair on a plinth in front of some graphics, Gary Lineker was in fact a dyed-in-the-wool socialist but with millions and millions of capitalist pounds. He proudly displayed a fierce dislike of Tories alongside a massive boner for social justice in general. Before long, his Twitter feed (as it was then known, though does *anybody* call it X? Centrist Dad certainly doesn't) read like the diary of a beret-wearing sixth-former who gets kettled by the police wearing a T-shirt that says FUCK OFF BORIS on it.

Soon the wider public were struggling to reconcile Centrist Dad TV presenter Gary with his post-millennial Wolfie Smithian alter-ego. By 2018 the once cuddly Gary had regularly begun to sound like Mick Lynch after a bad night's sleep. His outraged posts about immigration, the Middle East, Qatar's stance on LGBTQ rights, Brexit, the Rwanda deportation policy, Russian donors and the UK being mainly sewage began to piss off the section of his audience who don't like governments being nice to everyone, and so ever larger sections of his following began to turn on him.

Funnily enough, they pointed out, he had thus far managed to avoid getting outraged about the child obesity crisis (hello, crisps!): or, they observed, that he had accepted the job commentating on the Qatar World Cup whilst lording it over the government's culture of pretending homosexuality doesn't even exist. Gary had by now totally left the centre for the left, leaving half of his admirers sticking their vees up behind his now slightly sweatier shirt. And once that many eyes are trained on a person's every Tweet, the perception of their sense of balance is now, ironically enough, destined to walk a tightrope forever. Oh, Gary, it could have been so much simpler.

As this book goes to print Gary Lineker's *Match of the Day* persona has been totally exposed as a centrist mask, bought with seven-figure BBC contracts. But he fights on, trying to keep a break-water between X Gary, and, well, ex-Gary. The BBC even tried to suspend him but his studio pals downed tools and stood by their metal bins and warmed their hands for about 24 hours on his behalf. So for now, his lucrative contract and centrist mirage remain in front of us all, shimmering, though we all know it can't be there.

It is to be observed that there is *absolutely nothing wrong* with a person deciding that their true principles need to be brought out of the garage, polished up and ridden around the country roads wearing a headscarf and sunglasses. But in doing so that person must accept that they lose the ability to slip back behind the curtain of neutrality.

And therein lies the lesson for any Centrist Dad who is serious about his position, as a diplomatic, people-pleasing, Teflon voice of nothing-but-reason.

Maybe Gary Lineker is just a *really good guy*. Maybe it helps being politically brave at work when you have more money and crisps (and goals) than you could ever dream of behind you. This book does not seek to judge.

What is not in doubt is that whatever it is that Gary has which enables him to keep his good guy image afloat, Piers Morgan would probably swap a relative for it and then inject it into his own eyeballs.

And so, to all Centrist Dads who want to stay in their lane, it only remains to say this: whatever you do, learn everything you can from Lineker 1.0. Don't get booked. Iron your shirt. Stay neutral, but kind. And stay out of big, divisive debates* as much as humanly possible.

However, if you do want to unzip your charmingly neutral skinsuit and dance with the devil of passionately stated black-and-white opinion, drawing out the wolves from under their rocks with their fine-toothed microscopes, then the story of Lineker 2.0 has laid the narrative footsteps in which you can follow.

But always remember: deep in the darkened branches of the forest of righteous opinion lurk the glowing red eyes of the scorned, the left behind, the now-appearing-on-GB-News. And — who knows? — maybe even … Mark Lawrenson.

---

* And your brother's seedy Brits Abroad pub chain.

Centrist Dad's Playlist

Centrist Dad's playlist is a varied one (up to a point). He likes **Blur**, especially *Parklife,* but didn't want to take a side back in the days of the Britpop wars, so he also likes **Oasis**, especially *(What's The Story) Morning Glory?* He's fond of **Fatboy Slim, Massive Attack, Wyclef Jean, Air** (but just the one album – you know – the one everyone had), **The Chemical Brothers, R.E.M., Fun Lovin' Criminals, Girls Aloud** (and not solely for musical reasons), **Nirvana, Radiohead** (sometimes), **Joss Stone** and – these two are compulsory – **ABBA** and **The Beatles**.

But a lot of his musical knowledge runs out around 2007.

It's probably no coincidence that this is the year Tony Blair left office, and the centrist dream died a little. Then, just two days after Blair stepped down, the iPhone was launched, introducing the greatest distraction engine ever devised. And it may well be around this time that he was forced to put his music collection to one side in favour of albums like *Nursery Rhyme Time* and *My Favourite Animal Songs*. And when he did get a chance to dig out some **Pulp** or some **Beastie Boys**, he couldn't play anything too loud after 7 p.m. All of this put a huge hole in his musical world.

Beyond that date, though, one group has survived, digging its roots ever deeper into Centrist Dad's psyche. A group whose songs are tender, compassionate, gentle, sometimes sad, often witty, and always just beardy enough.

Elbow.

Guy Garvey conducting 5,000 weeping men in a heartfelt singalong.

The heartfelt love lyrics of Guy Garvey, sung in his sponge-cake voice, are enough to make Centrist Dad melt. That's how *he'd* tell someone he loved them if he could: he'd ask them to kiss him like a final meal. He'd say they kissed like they invented it. He'd tell them to kiss him nearly half to death. Instead, the best he manages is a breezy 'Love you!' and a peck on the lips as he leaves the house. He means it – of course he does – he just doesn't have the flair for anything more lyrical.

But Guy Garvey is the Poet Laureate of Centrist Dads, and Elbow is his delivery mechanism. And although the band has a working-class background, they're solidly middle class and wealthy now, meaning they are full spectrum, so their centre of gravity is exactly where Centrist Dad is. And besides, Guy Garvey's got a show on 6 Music, which automatically qualifies him as centrist.

Centrist Dad has seen Elbow live several times. They put on a great show, and can fill a big venue. And the sound is amazing.

However, Centrist Dad once made the mistake of going to **Glastonbury**. And while he enjoyed Elbow, he enjoyed literally no other element of the festival. He was expecting a weekend of good times, great music, a few beers and maybe a cheeky little something as a throw-back to his twenties.

Instead, he spent 48 excruciating hours in what seemed to be a temporary anarcho-socialist republic whose main policy goal was the destruction of farmland. Three quarters of the punters had never heard any music and were only there to wear wellies and headbands, like some weird outdoor cult. The zip on his tent broke and he had to tie the flaps back together with his right shoelace. And he was cornered in a field by gender-militant people on stilts.

Centrist Dad would, of course, much rather be at home with his **vinyl**. Since he got the Rega Planar 2 out of the loft, he's been playing lots of vinyl. He didn't have much vinyl back in the day, but fortunately, there are a lot of second-hand record shops sprouting up like dadnip – plus there are the record fairs, of course, where he can make small talk with the dealers who, thankfully, don't let their racist views stop them stocking Marvin Gaye and Nina Simone.

And, of course, there are the reissues on 180g vinyl. Centrist Dad makes sure he gets the shrink-wrapping off them as soon as (or before) they're home, so no-one sees how much he pays for them. But, he reassures himself, that copy of *OK Computer* actually sounds better *because* it cost £33. And that's the story he'll be sticking to when someone *does* spot the price tag.

At some point, he'll probably get his CDs out of the loft. Though he hasn't got anything to play them on. (And he'd definitely be spotted sneaking a £380 Marantz CD player into the house.) He's got a Manic Street Preachers MiniDisc somewhere, too, but he can't remember why.

One of these days, thinks Centrist Dad, he's going to pick up that guitar again. Maybe when the kids are older. He and some of his mates could hire a rehearsal studio and have a jam session. And then he thinks about how depressing the words *jam session* are, and how the prospect of stumbling through some covers, trying to remember the chords to something he last played twenty years ago, in a badly lit room haunted by the ghosts of 200,000 cigarettes, maybe isn't such a feelgood idea after all.

He'll probably just go back to Elbow. He knows where he is with them.

Centrist Dads
through History

Centrist Dad might seem like a recent phenomenon, like TikTok or Taylor Swift*, but in fact he has been around for as long as there have been dads.

Shakespeare, for instance, was a Centrist Dad. We can tell this from his writing. 'To be or not to be? That is the question' is a perfect example of centrism. If Shakespeare had been anything other than centrist, he'd have answered the question. 'To be. That is the answer' is how non-centrist Hamlet would have dealt with his existential dilemma, and we'd have been denied one of the greatest speeches in the English language. Another win for centrism. (On the other

---

* TikTok was launched in 2016 and Taylor Swift's first album was released in 2006, but both of these count as 'recent' to Centrist Dad, who still thinks kombucha is a new thing. Kombucha has been around for over 2,000 years.

hand, *Hamlet* is about five hours long, so non-centrist Shakespeare would have cut to the chase and spared his audience's arses a few aches.)

Likewise, **Henry Ford** was a Centrist Dad. The car had already been invented, but what Ford did was go one stage further and invent the *boring* car. 'Any colour you want as long as it's the colour I've chosen for you, which some people argue isn't even a colour anyway' is a great example of resolving a matter of choice in one hit. To this day, Ford has *never* made an interesting car, although the Corsair was a bit quirky and the Puma wasn't bad.

And Henry Ford was standing on the shoulders of giants, because **the Man who Invented the Wheel** was obviously a Centrist Dad. Anyone who can invent a *completely timeless thing with literally one side* is centrist through and through.

Dickens was another great Centrist Dad of yore. He was worried about the poor, and the terrible conditions of the Victorian workhouse, but being a good centrist (and not wanting to be thought of as anything as vulgar as an activist) he wrote about it instead of doing anything.

Neville Chamberlain was a Centrist Dad, but unfortunately at the exact moment when that was of absolutely no help whatsoever, because trying to negotiate with an actual Nazi is like bringing a cupcake to a knife fight.

Steve Davis, the snooker supremo turned unlikely DJ, is another. He was so famously centrist that he wouldn't even commit to an emotional state like happiness or being pleased when he won any of his six world titles.

Isaac Newton was a classic centrist (albeit never a dad). He just sat under a tree until an idea fell on his head. Strong centrist energy. (Although he might have argued it's only *potential* energy.)

The Green Cross Code Man was a first-rate Centrist Dad. He even helped other people's children across the road, like a Superdad. Sadly

Always look both ways before you cross over to The Dark Side.

he was radicalised in later life and went on to become Darth Vader, an Extremist Dad who tried to fight his own son to the death.

The jury's out on **Galileo**, unfortunately. He was right about the earth revolving around the sun, but Pope Urban VIII wasn't having any of it, instead holding to the belief that the earth was the centre of the solar system and that the sun revolved around it. So Galileo had to present both sides of the argument, which sounds like straight up-and-down centrism. But, counterpoint: if you're advocating being at the centre of the solar system, you're as centrist as it gets, even though you're wrong and should stick to Poping.

And there's **God**, obviously. The OG Centrist Dad. He allegedly created life, which might sound a bit authoritarian, but He then let us get on with it. Free will means it can't be His fault if there are worms that burrow through children's eyes: boss-level fence-sitting. (This is the New Testament God, obviously. The Old Testament one is fantastically pissed off and opinionated.)

Centrist Dad's Luggage

It might seem trivial, but luggage is everything. It says as much about its owner as his hair or clothes do, and Centrist Dad knows he is going to be judged on what he carries his laptop and his water bottle in. So he needs to get it right.

Centrist Dad has a **backpack**, like everyone else. (He may even have more than one. Scientists predict that by the year 2060 there will be more backpacks than people.) But it mustn't be either too swanky (like a Sandqvist or a Briggs & Riley) or look like something he'd take into the sea, and it shouldn't be some fraying bit of junk he's had since 1999. A sensible Eastpak will do. As long as it fits his MacBook and the tangled mess of charging cables he spends twenty minutes a day untangling (and vowing to tidy up), it's doing the job.

Also, his backpack must not be accessorised. Badges are for students, padlocks are for the paranoid and garlands are for Hawaiians. Centrist Dad is none of these things.

The first rule of Rucksack Club is you do not walk about without a rucksack.

Centrist Dad must also not own a briefcase, a hanky tied to an over-the-shoulder stick, a hatbox, anything ex-army, or one of those metal suitcases that looks like it either contains a load of needlessly expensive toiletries or a disassembled semi-automatic rifle packed into specially cut bits of foam.

One thing Centrist Dad must own is a **man bag**. Man bags used to be unacceptable, and any man carrying one was thought to be either suspiciously camp or shamelessly German. But something changed in the early 21st century, and man bags are now as socially acceptable as cockapoos or marshmallows in coffee.

Centrist Dad's man bag has only his essentials in it: his reading glasses, his chewing gum, his Airpods, his keys and his Anusol.

His **water bottle**, like everyone's, is getting bigger and bigger every time he replaces it. He will have to draw the line eventually, and it'll probably be at something the size of a fire extinguisher. Centrist Dad's back can only take so much – and it'll be less and less every year once he's over the hill.

The Centrist Dad
Coolness Spectrum

It can feel like pretty much everyone is on some sort of spectrum these days, but the one that seems to be most useful in measuring the inner workings of Centrist Dad is the Coolness Spectrum. This was created by the Centrism Faculty of Oxford Brookes University, and allows us to measure the perceived *and* actual coolness of male public cultural figures in real terms. The scale goes from 'woefully uncool' to 'so cool they are almost another species'.

This alignment tool is mercifully helping thousands of Centrist Dads set realistic goals for how cool or not cool they should attempt to be if they want to maintain their position safely in the middle of all the things that have ever happened.

The absolute sweet-spot, or dead-centre of the Coolness Spectrum, is almost impossible for anyone to achieve, but a few legendary figures have managed it, as visible on the chart below.

It's worth pointing out, though, that Centrist Dad's job is *not to be cool* and that neither coolness nor uncoolness should ever be his goal. The spectrum was created entirely for the purpose of raising awareness of how men can come across. Getting too familiar with it can lead to something called *self-awareness*, which is something Centrist Dad is not widely accepted to have that much of.

Centrist Dad should try not to be too harsh on himself when he sees where he feels he may fall on the coolness spectrum, though he is highly likely to see himself as *much* cooler than he actually is.

The guide's main use is for giving Centrist Dad an accurate reading as to where potential role models and man-muses may lie on the spectrum so that he can begin to give more thought to where he should realistically try to align himself. After all, there is little point trying to try and present yourself as having the beguiling determination of a Pep Guardiola in a Champions League Final if, in fact, you are giving off the vibe of a rain-sodden Nick Clegg hosting an ill-attended barbecue.

The Centrist Dad

| | AT LEAST YOU'RE COOLER THAN THIS LOT | | | THESE ARE | |
Woefully Uncool	Superdork	Full Dork	Think They Are Cool But Are a Mild Dork	So Uncool They Are Kind of Cool	Centrist
James Blunt's music	John Oliver	Robert Peston	Sadiq Khan	Jim Al-Khalili	**Keir Starmer**
Prince William	Mr Tumble	David Tennant	David Lammy	Henry The Vacuum Cleaner	**Gary Lineker**
Andy Murray	Gary fucking Barlow	Alistair Campbell	Gary Neville	Louis Theroux	**Martin Lewis**
	Nick Clegg	Rory Stuart	Greg Wallace	Paddington Bear	**Jermaine Jenas**
	Harry Potter	Dan Walker	James Martin	Gareth Southgate	
	Ed Balls (in reality)		Ed Sheeran	Pete Buttigieg	
	Jeremy Vine		Brian Cox (science version)	Jeff Stelling	

Coolness Spectrum

	YOUR GUYS		NOT GOING TO HAPPEN			
Sweetspot	**Almost Cool**	**Cool**	**Je Ne Sais Quoi Zone**	**Getting a Bit Too Cool for You**	**Don't Even Think About It**
Dermot O'Leary	Romesh Ranga-nathan	Justin Trudeau	Pep Guardiola	Stormzy	Skrillex
				Paul Weller	Reggie Yates
Larry The Downing Street Cat	Stephen Bartlett	Bill Nighy	Jon Stewart	The Grim Reaper	Alex Turner
	Peter Crouch	Idris Elba	Brian Cox (actor version)	Michael Kiwanuka	Harry Styles
John Lewis (the shop)		Marcus Rashford	James Blunt's tweets		Ncuti Gatwa
		Bradley Wiggins	Prince Harry		Sleaford Mods
		Hugh Grant	Ed Balls (in his own mind)		Top Cat
		Adam Buxton	Mark Owen		
			Thierry Henry		

Centrist Dad and Sport

According to research that nobody has actually needed to do because it's so painfully obvious already, Centrist Dads tend to be carrying a *lot* of pent-up negative energy, nervous tension and uncompressed, deeply submerged aggression. This is neither ideal nor sustainable.

It is believed that just one hour of the unfiltered anger generated by choosing to be the bigger person every waking second of the day is the equivalent in kilojoules of one angry first serve by Novak Djokovic. That's one repressed inner Krakatoa per day, eating away at Centrist Dad's guts. Just from trying to be nice.

But there is good news. Playing, watching and even just shouting at a sport is regarded as the number one way to healthily channel unacknowledged rage about all sorts of divisive issues such as 20mph speed limits, the sustainability of avocados and Dermot O'Leary.

Good news? Maybe not so much for Centrist Dad. On the surface the bland ubiquity of sport would appear to be a foolproof subject for Centrist Dad to navigate. What could be safer and less divisive than engaging with an entire category of human life that makes room for every single person's individual relationship with competitiveness, participation, strength, movement and endeavour?

If only it were so simple. The reality is that the world of sport exists within a complex hornet's nest of issues including class, gender, race, social status, privilege, prejudice, shouting and Lycra. Which is not to say that there are *no* sports that Centrist Dad can be seen engaging with, just that much like literally everything else, he must choose carefully or his egalitarian poise will be blown to smithereens.

Cycling

Cycling is both a sport *and* a word that scores highly in the Centriverse. After all, it literally means going round and round. Handily, both the wheels and the cyclist's legs do this continuously during the activity itself, making Centrist Dad feel at one with the inner circularity that defines his thinking. Even just cycling from A to B usually results in having to arrive back at A, which is often a garage. There is simply no single activity that defines Centrist Dad more completely than cycling, and for that reason it is without question his *number one* sport – whether participating, watching it on TV or writing defensive-sounding letters about it to broadsheet newspapers. All the big hitters in Centrist Dad's psyche are there: non-fossil-fuel mode of transport, safety equipment, hours of punishing, joyless focus and Lycra (again).

A velodrome is akin to a cathedral to Centrist Dad: a lottery-funded temple of circularity. On weekends all A-roads lead to a personal Damascus in the form of a very, very far away piece of cake with an equally ridiculous looking Centrist Dad on an even more expensive bike. This ritual allows for the clocking-up of terrifying-sounding distances that he can show off about to his colleagues at work, blissfully unaware that literally nobody gives a single shit.

As we all know, just like a vegan, a cyclist is a cyclist 24/7, 365 days a year, and as such it is during the week that the self-satisfaction of walking into his office dripping with sweat having already done his exercise before 9am is almost impossible for him to process without being reduced to floods of salty tears. Perhaps this is why Centrist Dad always looks a bit red-faced and unapproachable after he emerges from the shower at work.

Athletics

Athletics is another word that represents an immediate sports win for Centrist Dad. Saying you are a fan of athletics is like saying your favourite place to go on holidays is *destinations,* which is the kind of non-opinion opinion that Centrist Dad can get behind.

Finding just one word that covers 42 hugely diverse Olympian sporting events is the linguistic equivalent of a Westfield Shopping centre food court. It is beautifully vague, whilst sounding specific. It is plural, and therefore pluralistic (yum) and it evokes the sight of a stadium full of people from around the world (none of whom are lager-fuelled hooligans) watching athletes of all kinds running, throwing various differently shaped objects, spinning around in a cage and jumping into sandpits all at the same time.

As a spectacle, the average Olympic athletics day has more in common with a Where's Wally poster than, say, an FA Cup quarter-final replay, so it is perfectly reasonable to root for everybody involved, including whoever comes last. There may be allegiances of an international nature, but everyone always cheers the best one. And, marvellously, most of the outcomes are reached by volunteers in blazers measuring things wearing a white butcher's trilby. Absolutely harmless.*

This gruelling squash game between Centrist Dad and himself ended in a draw.

---

* Apart from all the performance-enhancing drugs. But then again, let's not get started on them and cycling.

Ball Games

We now approach lumpier terrain as we contemplate the various sports whose central protagonist is a sphere. Or, in rugby's case, a large leatherette egg.

It would be tempting to believe that all ball games are essentially the same thing. After all, they are often based on the shared principle that balls tend to roll and can be moved through the air by humans. *Do not be fooled.* Culturally and socially, there is nothing more divisive in the sporting arena than the exact type of ball you personally prefer to see being smacked about.

Centrist Dad should be in no doubt that aligning to a ball game is like signing up to a political party whose manifesto he hasn't read. If he does not know what he is doing or saying, he may end up breezily joining in with an offensive song about someone's anus, or eating cucumber sandwiches in a boardroom that does not allow women in without a Hoover.

So how should Centrist Dad navigate the tricky ubiquity of the Ball Game?

RUGBY

Even more than other sports, rugby presents tricky class-based issues. If Centrist Dad is going to engage with rugby he *must* remember to try and pay both rugby union (middle- to upper-class) and rugby league (mainly working-class) the same level of attention. This is tricky and psychologically not unlike toggling between a vegan supermarket and an abattoir. The rules differ slightly, with the league version encouraging pacey use of the wingers and tactical guile whilst literally having no neck and a thick Northern accent, whilst union is more about wearing an expensive private school's tie around one's head whilst otherwise naked, having necked 37 pints of Doom Bar.

FOOTBALL

Association football was originally invented so that the overstretched police forces of industrial Britain's cities could put all of the mass brawls that were plaguing the country into their diaries on Saturday afternoon at 5 p.m. The (then) entirely working-class crowd would save up their pennies and their anger at being crammed into factories that mainly made smog, and release it at the game by swearing whilst wearing a flat cap.

One hundred and fifty years later, modern football is still the number one release valve for the working classes, but now it costs £80 a ticket so the crowd is even angrier. This is not helped by the availability of cheap cocaine, Danny Dyer films and *Peaky Blinders* hats.

At the other end of the scale, around a third of a modern football crowd is made up of middle-class corporate schmoozers, paying up to £300 per ticket, none of whom know the words to any football songs and who watch the game from toughened-glass balconies whilst being served pan-fried hake and crushed minted potatoes on a roofing slate from what used to be the main stand. Meanwhile, on the pitch, even bang-average players are now often cossetted multimillionaires by the time they are seventeen, and most of the major clubs and competitions are sponsored by energy companies, airlines and oppressive regimes.

So where can Centrist Dad possibly fit into this rampant capitalist nightmare?

Well, he can start by never accepting a glass of wine at any match he may attend unless it is in the team manager's office. He mustn't cheer or boo. Clapping and nodding is more than enough. He must remember to never wear a replica shirt with chinos or fool himself that he can carry off a Stone Island jumper worth £800. Most importantly, he must *never* switch teams.

When all's said and done, it's best for Centrist Dad to just quietly watch the football from his sofa while hoping for a 3–3 thriller he can talk about in the pub for months. In that event, if asked by the rougher boys who he supports, he should say that he keeps an eye on his local team but has lost interest a bit since all the oil money got involved. He might want to try this phrase: 'for me, the Premiership peaked during the Ferguson/Wenger era, they're all wankers now,' and then change the subject to which was the best-ever Dennis Bergkamp goal before leaving early because he has to be up in the morning.

CRICKET

Every single male attending the average cricket match will very likely look like a classic Centrist Dad, and for that reason cricket is probably the least risky sport for him to try and play or follow (unless he is hit by the ball in which case he will die instantly). All Centrist Dad has to do is turn up anywhere where there is some cricket and he will instantly dissolve into a wall of his bland, quietly competitive brethren. Sounds simple enough, but there are some sinister things to look out for in the world of cricket, most of which have come out of Geoffrey Boycott's mouth at some point.

When all is said and done, outside England, cricket is played almost exclusively by countries that had the game forced upon them by handlebar-moustached members of the British Empire during brief intervals in ravaging their nations. As such, it should be troubling to any fair-minded man that the map of participating nations in even the 2023 Cricket World Cup looks exactly like the one that Queen Victoria had on her tea-towels.

On the plus side, the average game of cricket can take place over such a stultifyingly long time that nobody really cares who has won and who has lost because nobody since Oliver Reed can handle being on the piss that long. This means the blind, ugly hatred that fills the air in a football stadium is thankfully replaced by polite smatterings of occasional applause that can easily be drowned out by a fork hitting the china plate beneath a slice of lemon drizzle cake. This lack of venom makes a perfect environment for Centrist Dad to saunter around in and he should relish taking this opportunity to enjoy himself, whilst making sure that he avoids wearing a straw boater or saying anything from 1971.

All the Other Ones

There are literally dozens of other sports but none of them are even vaguely suitable for Centrist Dad for the following reasons.

American Football has too much junk food, too many adverts, and a half-time entertainment budget higher than the GDP of a developing country: no place for Centrist Dad.

Basketball is not inclusive enough across the height spectrum. Having to be *seven feet tall* to play a sport is frankly ludicrous. Until basketball decides to include different height divisions, the way boxing does with weight, it must be boycotted or kept to his own front drive.

Tennis couldn't be more loaded in favour of the well-off if it was only played exclusively on the helicopter decks of supervillains' yachts. If Centrist Dad wants to use a racket he must play **Swingball** or **table tennis** on his own, with one side of the table up.

The role of **gymnastics** in Centrist Dad's life should be this: wait in the car while his children do the gymnastics.

Surfing, windsurfing, kite surfing, wakeboarding and **just looking cool on a jet-ski** are best left to muscular, blonde-looking types from Australia or Cornwall. Centrist Dads of lesser stock should back away now.

Centrist Dad is a respectful and gentle lover, not a fighter. The only **combat sport** even vaguely appropriate for him is **judo**. This is because judo is basically taking responsibility for another person's aggression (and their weight) whilst rolling around the floor while wearing pyjamas. Lovely.

Other than snowball fights and sliding down a snowy hill in the park inside a binbag once a year there are no **winter sports** that are available to anybody even vaguely centrist. It's best to leave this sort of stuff to unhappily married royals and James Bond.

Frankly the same rules as above apply to **rowing**. Centrist Dad's only morally acceptable options here are either a rowing machine bolted to a floor in front of a mirror, or two Centrist Dads in a double kayak, rowing towards each other. See picture.

As for the following, just don't:

- Luge
- The Eton Wall Game
- Pheasant Plucking
- Lamping
- Bareknuckle Boxing
- Badger Baiting
- The Dogs
- Croquet
- Dressage
- Joyriding

The Philosophy of Adrian Chiles

Centrist Dad's philosopher of choice is Adrian Chiles. His vague, harmless musings on his teenage kids, his shopping habits and his beloved West Brom excite no strong feelings, not even among Villa fans. Some of his best-read columns include:

Nothing you can say will ever change my mind about Shreddies

If you asked me to choose between nuclear war and VAR, I'd have to get back to you

Yet again, there's someone tall in front of me

Why can't everything be circular? There'd be less cleaning to do

I spent the entire weekend in the bath and now I can't stand being dry

Is it me getting bigger or is bread
getting smaller?

I heard a cat bark and my therapist
doesn't believe me

The Mr Men could teach us all a thing or
two about breakfast and I should know

My kids watch people ironing on TikTok
and apparently this is normal

I've started making up songs about parking
and I think I'm on to something

How can soup be a food and a drink at
the same time?

There's nothing unreasonable about
wanting a second front door

If nectarines are interchangeable with
satsumas, I'm a Dutchman

If thermostats could talk, mine would
have its own chat show

Three years on and I still don't have
a favourite houmous

Adrian Chiles making one of his points.

You can't even sit on a urinal in a pub
toilet these days without someone
calling the police

If I had a pound for every two-pound
coin I've got in my pocket right now,
I'd have three pounds

I've started cleaning the grouting in my
shower with toothpaste for some reason

I've put my entire music collection in
the cellar and filled it with concrete.
Don't ask me why

We can put a man on the moon, but
I can't buy takeaway toast

After a lot of practice, I can now tut
louder than I can shout

I was a dyed-in-the-wool gravity fan
until I bought a jetpack

My wife's gone to Pets At Home and
I'm not sure she's coming back

In my book, being found inside the
dishwasher is not a reason to have to
sleep on the sofa

If I could go back in time, I'd go back
to the beginning of this sentence and
not write it

I once welcomed year-round access
to strawberries, but now summer
means nothing to me

I only meant to drop my wife off at the
airport, but now I've been here three days

I'm almost certain my dog
understands snooker

'Bionic wrath wombles' is an anagram of
West Bromwich Albion. Coincidence?

Automatic windscreen wipers have
taken all the fun out of turning on the
windscreen wipers

Don't ask me why, but I've just put an
entire jigsaw down the waste disposal

Centrist Dad and Art

Centrist Dad has a complicated relationship with art. This isn't his fault: there isn't much centrist art. Artists tended to be paid shills of the rich and entitled (very uncentrist in one direction) or radicals determined to rip up the status quo and shit all over it (even more uncentrist, in the other direction).

So whose work can Centrist Dad endorse, and who must he avoid?

Well, he's safe with a **Rothko**, because it's just shapes and slabs of colour, and all rather agreeable. Plus, his first name was Mark, which is nice and centrist.

Monet is a good steer too, because it's basically just water lilies. And what could be more centrist than a flower that *doesn't* show off and just floats?

Picasso – forget it. He can't even centre a nose.

Dalí – definitely not, because Centrist Dad has decided that the only time it's permissible to bend reality is when nipping an argument in the bud.

Van Gogh is difficult. He was OK when he had two ears. But after that, nope.

Kahlo – loves her. She's the acceptable surrealist. (Plus, he fancied Selma Hayek in the movie.)

Lowry is one he tries to avoid, because even though his depictions of the working class are authentic, Centrist Dad worries that if he starts saying nice things about the pictures, people will think he's being patronising – especially since (and he'll never admit this) *he can't work out if Lowry was any good*. This is the same reason he avoids all tapestry.

When it comes to the **YBAs**, he thought the *Sensation* exhibit was fantastic. He didn't actually *go* to it, but he liked that it was an exciting time and even though he thinks Damien Hirst and Tracy Emin are rubbish, he appreciates what they did for British art. (He used to have a Chapman brothers print in a frame, but it's in the loft now, and he keeps quiet about the time he once took ecstasy with someone who said he was Damien Hirst.)

Luckily, Centrist Dad has a big hitter on his side: the **Mona Lisa**. He loves it. It's absolutely perfect for him, because it's the most boring painting in the world. (And she's not enigmatic, she's just not committing to any one emotional position. Classic centrism.) Plus, it's popular, uncontroversial, and not too big. It's just a shame it's in France. Luckily, he's seen it so many times, he can just close his eyes and see it without having to go there.

Seeing the Mona Lisa in real life is a haunting experience: the iPhones really follow you around the room.

How to Deal with a Crisis

There are times when trying to do and say the right thing gets all too much for Centrist Dad, and he might find himself having an uncharacteristic outburst. This might take the form of a low-level aggression like not rinsing out a milk bottle properly – or he may go 'Full Clarkson' and make a bonfire of all the books and clothes he's been meaning to take to Oxfam for three months.

When this happens, and especially if Centrist Dad has done something like eaten six packets of Haribo and arranged the magnetic letters on the fridge to read BURN THIS SHIT EARTH, it may be a cry for help.

Luckily for Centrist Dad, there are places he can realign himself with his values – retreats like Himfulness in Surrey, run by the Centrist Dad Re-Centring Centre, where he can go for what's affectionately known as a 'Woking awokening'.

Centrist Dad sometimes gets to relax like this for up to twelve seconds before someone needs some money for something.

The activities at Himfulness include Sunrise Tutting, the Never-Mind Circle and the always popular Smash-Up Therapy, where the Centrist Dads paint '£350m' on the side of an old bus before smashing it to fucking pieces with their fists and heads.

Himfulness uses a 'forbidden rewards' system. Clients are first encouraged to relax some of their core values in a safe space, in return for which they are allowed indulgences.

For example, to honour the personal sacrifice in the name of the planet of minimising the amount of processed meat they eat, the Dads take turns sitting in a bath full of sausages and crying.

There are also structured raging sessions. The Centrist Dads are carefully whipped up into a frenzy about crisp shrinkflation, indistinct TV dialogue, blue headlights, not being able to peel open bacon packaging, dishwashers that don't dry stuff properly, potholes in cycle lanes, Pret coffee being too hot, seeing 'alot'' written as one word, having to download yet another Zoom update when you're meant to be in the meeting already, self-service checkouts treating you like a shoplifter if you put your Bag For Life on the scale with anything heavier than a packet of dill in it — and, for the Centrist Dad who struggles to make contact with his anger, there's a special soundproofed room where he can listen to the Joey Barton podcast.

Centrism Won't
Help You Now

There are times when centrism is no help at all. This presents a tricky situation for Centrist Dad, because his relied-upon methods of negotiating life (with ease, balance and moderation) fail him.

For instance: **shark attack.** It is difficult to compromise with a shark. In fact, it's difficult to even *see things* from the shark's point of view. Being attacked by a shark is, of course, political, because the shark is an extremist. But since there is no way of establishing the shark's precise political leanings as the teeth sink into Centrist Dad's legs, there is no chance to form a coherent argument as to why the huge creature shouldn't treat him as a meal deal.

Nobody likes to admit they deserve their **parking ticket** but 99.9 per cent of the time, that is the case. With this in mind, it is better for Centrist Dad to accept he is a human being that

Yes, it's majestic, and yes, it's magnificent, but you're not going to reason your way out of it eating you.

fucked up, twat the steering wheel a few times, pay the fine and move on. He may not want to hear it but going to extraordinary lengths to try and plead the case for his excellent previous parking record or against a conspiratorial universe that meant he 'couldn't possibly' have seen the road-sign or the big painted yellow lines is a monumental waste of his energy. Also, perhaps Centrist Dad could spare a thought for the poor bugger who has to deal with 43 other Centrist Dads' letters per day hoping to finally be the one who brings the system crashing down with his tear-jerking explanation that he 'only nipped into Boots for two minutes to pick up a prescription for his ailing mother'.

An extreme example, and one Centrist Dad is not likely to come up against, is if someone points a **gun** at his face.* Centrism, despite its many qualities, is no match for a bullet, and anyone intending to fire one is probably a long way from nodding in quiet agreement at something reasonable. It's also not a good idea for Centrist Dad to point out to his armed potential assailant that he should have issued a trigger warning first. It's better all-round if Centrist Dad takes this opportunity to shut the fuck up.

The same attitude can be beneficial to Centrist Dad's health in a situation where he finds himself casually wandering into the middle of some **football hooliganism**. It may seem reasonable to argue that two sets of men living and working in the same city have no legitimate reason to throw plastic chairs and traffic cones at each other on the basis that they have chosen to support a team that wears a particular colour. The important thing to remember is that the concourse of Euston Station, at the moment when forty Tottenham fans spot their Chelsea

---

* Obviously, if he's particularly irritating, it could lead here. It's probably best he winds his neck in now and then, just to be on the safe side. Everyone has a breaking point.

rivals outside Wetherspoons, is not the time to try and start the healing. Run very away. *Now*.

Viruses don't respond well to centrism either. Centrist Dad had little helpful to offer during the COVID-19 pandemic (even washing his hands, which was *by definition* even-handed, proved to be useless) and he has just as little to offer when he or someone in the family gets a cold. Unless you count tissues.

Another charmingly dangerous foe is a **house fire.** The problem with fire is that it's *strictly egalitarian*, and therefore basically centrist itself. And you can't fight centrism with centrism. So for Centrist Dad to fight a fire, he'd have to abandon all his carefully held political opinions and assume an anti-centrist position. It is better for Centrist Dad to step away from a house fire, and leave the Fire Brigade to deal with it.

As we know, Centrist Dad loves being supportive and that's OK. However, generously giving the benefit of the doubt to the line of screaming workmen who are trying to stop him **driving at high speed towards the end of an unfinished bridge** is a silly idea: as lovely as it is for him to show such faith in a workforce that he believes they will finish the job before he reaches the end of the bridge, he might in this instance want to consider slamming the brakes on and giving them another four months to sort it out. Furthermore he should note that in the event that he does decide to plough on towards the not-roady bit of the structure, it is almost certain that there isn't going to be a four-second pause where he hangs momentarily in the air with his feet spinning around to the sound of bongos. This is one moment where extreme caution is a very good option.

On safer ground, should Centrist Dad find himself at an **auction** bidding for a guitar once played by the Edge from U2 that would really set off the space next to the reclaimed driftwood mirror in his study, he would do well to note that lowering his bid to give the others a chance, or pointing out people who are waving their brochures around him to the auctioneer, is only going to cost him a prize bit of rock ephemera in the long run.

Walking confidently towards a newly arrived, gang-plank-descending representative of an **alien invasion** with a potted tomato is a lovely gesture. But it also the carries the distinct risk that Centrist Dad is going to be immediately stabbed in the eyes with the visitor's mutant sword-appendage. Wanting to set a peaceful tone is absolutely fine, but first smiles and welcoming arms should be deployed from a distance longer than the standard length of the average rapidly protruding xenomorph-tongue.

If Centrist Dad finds himself invited to a **gangster rap lyric-writing brainstorm**, he should try to remember to sit back and non-judgementally observe the rhythmic and aural aspects of some of the more troubling sentiments being scrawled onto the A-Board in marker pen. He should do this for at least half an hour *before* he starts to deconstruct them from a male feminist point of view. There will be a little more trust in the room for his reason-infused rhymes if he can demonstrate that he is a gang member himself. However, it's best not to try and present his connections to his badminton or running club as having equivalence with a well-known drill crew who control the flow of Class A drugs into their ends until *well* after lunch.

One time of the year when it is best to hang up one's Centrist principles and just keep a low profile is **Christmas fucking dinner.** Everybody in attendance is already fully aware that Centrist Dad thinks that GB News has poisoned his mother's already fascistic mind, but all everyone wants to do on the day is eat the turkey, pull the crackers and get the hell out of there before the screaming matches start. One way to head this off is to drink a whole bottle of the most Centrist Drink available (50/50 Bucks Fizz) before 9am to get into the 'la la la not rising to it' mindset as soon as possible.

Finally, sorry to tell you, but **time** waits for no man, including Centrist Dad. The rotten news is he too is going to get even older and very probably slightly less Centrist from here on in. The best he can hope for is that the dwindling sands of the time he has left don't shorten his admirably long fuse and turn him into the dreaded Gestapo Grandad that lurks inside him.

Centrist Dad Goes
to the Movies

Centrist Dad loves the movies as much as anyone, but as he has matured and become more and more enlightened, he has started to find the strong adult themes of some of cinema's greatest titles a little too rich for his tastes. But fear not, because as his mild-mannered sensibility has spread through the country like room-temperature organic butter, many of his favourite films have been re-dubbed, re-edited and even re-shot for the Centrist Dad market. All of the following are available to stream on Dadflix.

Half-and-half sweet and salty popcorn, of course.

- *Some Like It Tepid*

- *The Medium Lebowski*

- *Star Negotiations*

- *The Goodfather Trilogy*

- *The Qualified Doctor of Oz*

- *Donnie Dusko*

- *My Left Foot (and My Right Foot)*

- *Sophie's Indecision*

- *No Country for Middle-Aged Men*

- *Shaun of the Unwell*

- *Apocalypse Eventually*

- *A.T. – The Average Terrestrial*

- *Twelve Agreeable Men*

- *Two Flew Over the Cuckoo's Nest*

- *Southeast by Northwest*

- *Sales Reps of the Caribbean*

- *Where Eagles Wait to See How It Pans Out*

- *Blade Jogger*

- *Saving PFI Ryan*

- *Respectable Me*

- *The Good, the Bad and the Making Progress in Rehabilitation*

- *To Spot a Mockingbird*

- *Try Hard*

- *Curators of the Lost Ark*

- *Half Metal Gilet*

- *Bike Club*

- *Dorky Dancing*

- *Not Bad Will Hunting*

- *Rehoming Nemo*

- *The Credibles*

- *Come to an Agreement With Bill, Vol.1*

- *Toy Story 1.5*

- *Things To Do in Denver When You're There for a Conference*

- *Cautiousheart*

- *Goatscheesebusters*

- *Ferris Bueller's Work Experience*

Centrist Dad's
Guide to Winning
an Argument

Arguing with Centrist Dad can be difficult. Someone who refuses to take sides isn't really worth arguing with. But that's how Centrist Dad likes it. An argument-free world is a peaceful one.

Except ... people who refuse to take sides are also, to many more opinionated types, infuriating. So Centrist Dad needs to be ready for the full-on assault of the opinionated and know how to assuage their fury. Some of the following phrases may prove useful for him:

There's always a happy compromise to be found.[*]

---

[*] This is bollocks.

[Witnessing a punch-up] I'm sure there are merits in what both these people are trying to kill each other about.

To quote Bill Clinton, 'Not left, or right, but forward.'*

Let's see how this one pans out.

What if we're both right? Or both wrong?

I hear what you're saying. *[Add nothing after this unless repeating that phrase.]*

What would Gary Lineker say?

Let's just go back a couple of steps to before we started this conversation.

Can I just stop you there? *[Then say nothing more. There. They have been stopped.]*

---

* Appallingly smug.

So what you're saying makes sense in a four-dimensional world, but science currently postulates the existence of twenty-two.*

Would you rather I was Owen Jones/ Piers Morgan/Jeremy Corbyn *[delete as applicable]*?**

---

* Don't try this on a known physicist.
** This is unusually pass-agg for Centrist Dad. Careful. He might be in one of his moods.

Centrist Dad's Eleven Commandments

1. Thou shalt not waver from the centre by more than one millimetre lest anyone see you are a human being.

2. Thou shalt not take the name of LORD Starmer in vain. Yet. Depending on how he does with the big stuff over his first term.

3. Thou shalt not commit too eagerly to anything lest you be found contradicting yourself later in a way that makes the rest of the family cheer and mock thee.

4. Thou shalt not cancel thyself by speaking inner truths that went out of fashion in 2007.

5. Thou shalt not kill the buzz by
not allowing everyone their own
opinion over dinner.

6. Remember bin day and keep the colour
coding system HOLY because
they just introduced the food bins.

7. Thou shalt remember to keep
Sunday for cycling a very long way wearing
Lycra with other red-faced Centrist Dads
of a similar age.

8. Thou shalt honour thy mother
and father by placing an absolute ban
on discussing politics or having any TV
news channel on over Christmas.

9. Thou shalt not steal opinions from Alastair
Campbell nor Rory Stewart and try to pass
them off as thine own.

10. Thou shalt not covet thy
neighbour's superfast broadband,
nor their bike shed.

11. Thou shalt add an 11th commandment reserving the right to review thy position on the 10 commandments upon robust new information coming to light.

12. Thou shalt not end on an 11th commandment so that there may not be an indivisible number of commandments.

Centrist Dad's
Guide to Jobs

Centrist Dad has to pay the bills, and the rocketing price of olive oil means pesto isn't cheap these days.

But how? Some jobs are better suited to him than others.

For instance, he'd make an excellent **gardener**. People like their bushes and trees to be basically symmetrical, and nobody has extreme opinions about plants. (In fact, very few people have any opinions about plants at all.)

Whereas **referee** or **umpire** is a terrible idea. Having to make decisions in favour of one side over the other *again and again* under stressful competition standards is the sort of thing that could give Centrist Dad a tension headache, a nosebleed, or the shits. Not for him a life of sporting judgement.

Likewise, Centrist Dad would make a terrible **Home Secretary**, because he'd inevitably introduce a third criminal verdict, midway between Guilty and Not Guilty, and call it something like Nobody's Perfect. Nor would he make a good **optician**, because constantly asking, 'is it better with … or without?' would grind poor Centrist Dad's gears something terrible.

But he'd be an excellent **barber**. The combination of third-party grooming and harmless conversation would suit Centrist Dad very well. Plus, he gets an enormous sense of well-being surrounded by sharp objects he means to put only to good purpose, as he knows from his time in the power tools section of Wickes.

Sam has never looked back since deciding to call his barber shop Centre Parts.

Obviously, he can't do **anything in hi-vis**. Although if Centrist Dad were presented with a hi-vis gilet, it might give off such strong confused signals that it would blow his mind. And he can't be a **taxi driver**, because everything about the job is right-wing, including where you sit to do it.

Centrist Dad would be great as **the person in the sandwich factory who cuts them in half**, but that's probably a job now taken by a centrist machine. In fact, there are plenty of jobs he could do which are now mechanised: **folding greetings cards**, for instance. Or folding anything, for that matter.

You'd think Centrist Dad would make an excellent **tightrope walker** – it's the very definition of what he does on the ground. The problem is, doing that (a) where it's risky and (b) performatively makes the whole thing too stressful. If there was such a thing as a ground-based tightrope walker, he'd be just the man for the job. But the highwire version is just too risky for Centrist Dad. He doesn't do balance *and danger* at the same time. It's for similar reasons that he's not a **member of the Olympic bobsleigh team.**

On the other hand, manning the decks on an internet-based MOR radio station is very much up Centrist Dad's street. As **DJ Centrist Dad**, he can play a wide variety of harmless music (his beloved Elbow, of course – but also Springsteen, R.E.M., John Grant, U2, Crowded House, The Beautiful South, Keane, Dido, Seal, Coldplay, Stereophonics, Travis, etc.) and, as it's an internet station, there are about 20 people listening, so his opinions – if, by some *terrible* accident he expresses any – don't gain any traction.

Centrist Dad's Guide to Things That Aren't OK Anymore

'Life moves pretty fast,' as Ferris Bueller once told us when we were all much bouncier and still full of the kind of fun and hopeless optimism that our children now drive us insane with. And how right he was: that was somehow over thirty-five fucking years ago, rather proving his point, but what even Ferris wasn't able to predict was the speed at which some things that were broadly popular and acceptable for several uneventful decades would suddenly become *so offensive* that you would think that they must have happened when people were still drowning witches or sending urchins up chimneys.

These days it pays for Centrist Dad *never* to assume anything is OK anymore, and though there is no doubt that he has long ago got his head and heart around the kind of stuff that used to make it into episodes of *It Ain't Half Hot Mum*, he may be grateful for the following list of some slightly more obscure phenomena that Centrist Dad must now graciously leave behind with his frayed bootcut jeans and his iPod.

DOING A FUN RUN DRESSED AS A WOMAN

Time was when only an absolute pub legend had the balls* to pull on a pair of stockings and suspenders, shove a pair of balloons up an over-size blouse and go hammering around the local

This has not been OK since Kenny Everett died.

---

* Another phrase worth swerving.

park in a pair of Reeboks and rouge lipstick to raise £100 for Barnardo's. Nowadays they would be likely to return the cheque and do a terse social media post putting about a billion miles between their values and his.

EVOKING 'THE GIMP'

None of us know quite where we were when we first heard the term *kink-shaming*, but we have since got to know the feeling of trying to keep a straight face when someone in a social setting (an actual social setting) mentions their penchant for ball-gags, rubber masks and bollock-trampling, lest we be accused of trying to humiliate them for their preferences.* Let's just say it's probably best to not put *Pulp Fiction* on in polite company.

SCHOOL DISCOS

Now stop there. Nobody is questioning whether Centrist Dad would be foolish enough to want to stick around at a dreadful night where a load of thirteen-year-old TikTok addicts jump around to 'Gangnam Style' until they vomit Prime out of their nostrils. No,

---

* And yet, isn't that the whole point?

we are talking about the trend of fully grown adults attending club-nights in order to get drunk and flirt with each other while wearing outfits that were until not long ago printed in tabloid newspapers almost daily until everyone realised how deeply fucked up that was. In case you haven't got the memo: DO NOT ARRANGE A SCHOOL DISCO FANCY DRESS NIGHT. IT'S WEIRD.

THE FRAMED *MANHATTAN* POSTER THAT USED TO HANG IN THE HALLWAY

Yes, it once meant so much to him, and it was so beautifully photographed. He knew the movie was a visual love letter to Fellini and a sign that he expected cinema to make him think, as well as laugh. But the older he got, and the younger the leading lady seemed, the more it began to feel like he might as well be advertising a Bangkok go-go bar called Sugar Bunny, right next to where his kids take their shoes off, and quite rightly it began to trouble him. There is now a big art deco mirror there, thank God.

1/3 OF MONTY PYTHON AND
1/2 OF PINK FLOYD

Yes, the music and the comedy still hold up. No, nobody develops, commissions or even tries to make popular art to anywhere near this standard anymore. But now Centrist Dad must feel a bit sad as he slides either of these two peerless influences on his taste off the shelf to try and enjoy as once he did, because now he knows the DVD or CD he holds in his hand was made by groups of men you can no longer love in their entirety because *some of them* have become so bloodcurdlingly awful and bitter that it reminds you of watching Bruce Banner turn into the Hulk, but slower. And let's not even talk about the Smiths.

HELIUM BALLOONS

For many years helium balloons were as omnipresent as dandelions and were as essential to creating any sort of celebratory atmosphere as Champagne in plastic cups, and clapping. Except, of course, they weren't essential at all. They were dreadfully wasteful. Then, in a turn of events that the floaty gas itself can hardly complain about, helium's price went way up. Which is just as well because really it is needed for properly important stuff like MRI scanners rather than for making the number 50 float about looking a bit pissed. Think of it like this: one man's helium balloon is another's undiagnosed herniated disc.

MOST OF THE GOOD STUFF
FROM THE 90s

Frankly, there's not much left that you are still allowed to like from the 90s, even though Gen Z has fetishised its aesthetics in the exact same way the 90s movers and shakers fetishised the 60s and 70s. Baggy jumpers, bucket hats and massive flares may be floating around Centrist Dad's house with teenage children in them, but he shouldn't take that as his cue to pull out his Jo Guest edition of *Loaded*, whilst cueing up *Natural Born Killers* on the DVD player and dropping an E with Mum, because Gen Z will understandably *not* be OK with that. Frankly, he shouldn't even risk an episode of *Friends* these days without a written trigger warning.

REFERRING TO RUMOURS AS
'CHINESE WHISPERS'

This is the sort of linguistic turd-plonk that will catch even the most diligent Centrist Dad out purely on the grounds that he likely hasn't had a reason to use the term more than once every seven years or so. Well, a lot can change in seven years, including the sensitivity around assigning a nationality to a now worn-out phrase that hints at pernicious untrustworthiness. What's more, he should not bother trying to justify it based on an article he read about how Chinese technology is recording us at all times because *that's not why he said it*. The phrase 'Russian interference' is still fine, though. Some things, at least, are sacred.

THE FIRST 27 BOND FILMS

Loving Bond with a quintessentially British tongue in one's cheek was, until not long ago, as innocent an act as coveting a racing green MG Midget. Except convertible classic cars haven't got a habit of sleeping with about three women per hour before either slapping them or throwing them out of a window into a hotel swimming pool for talking a bit while he is looking for something. Until Daniel Craig, it may never have occurred to the average Centrist Dad to think about whether he would be deleting James Bond from his phone for being a wrong 'un if he was real. But then, one idle Sunday, he attempted to put an old classic 007 movie on to watch with the kids and the scales began to fall from his eyes. It then became clear that James Bond was possibly the worst role model ever. The character's epic misogyny totally obliterated the fact that he had always worked for whoever was in power, no questions asked. Let's hope the next version doesn't step back onto the Robin Thicke bus.

CHRIS MOYLES

Yeah. That whole episode hasn't aged well, has it?

Centrist Dad's No-Nos

The world is only getting more judgemental, and fast. And although it is, naturally, *vitally* important that all Centrist Dads are seen to be faultlessly non-judgemental about how other people choose to spend their time, right across the full class and culture spectrum of modern Britain, there are also some things which, while not exactly cancelled and perfectly fine for some people, are nevertheless to be avoided by Centrist Dad.

Living one's daily life should feel as seamless as running a string of pearls through a gentle folded hand, but in the world of Centrist Dad, every decision – every individual act – carries within it the dark shadow of the threat of accidentally aligning himself with people to the left *and* to the right of him.

This can result in accidental inappropriateness, folly, faux-pas and *fucking hell what's happened to Steve?* If Centrist Dad is serious about his centrism, something as simple as loading a set of golf clubs into the boot of a prestige saloon car has now to be considered via the prism of *optics*, lest he lose his aura of impenetrable uber-goodness forever.

With that in mind, here is a non-exhaustive list of things that a Centrist Dad must never ever be seen doing.

Attending a Ricky Gervais stand-up gig, especially if it's going to be on Netflix

Buying anything from Edinburgh Woollen Mill

Being seen speaking through a loud hailer in Trafalgar Square

Being helped into an overcoat at the Reform Club

Lying under an Austin Princess in a boiler suit

Spreading anything from Fortnum & Mason on an oatcake

Singing a Billy Bragg song at an open mic night

Nipping to Biarritz in a Learjet

Watching *The Hunger Games* whilst cupping his balls

Doing the *Telegraph* crossword on a train wearing a bowler hat

Signing a hysterical petition from a friend's Instagram story

Being shown around a Chinese factory in a hard hat

Spurring on a colleague to batter a business rival at a white-collar boxing event

Throwing a bikini-clad promo girl into a swimming pool

Playing five-a-side with Mick Lynch and the lads

Donating a bottle of 2004 Puligny-Montrachet to the school fair's bottle tombola

Jumping around the mosh pit of a Chumbawumba gig

Smoking a cigar on a yacht whilst proudly displaying a huge belly, surrounded by Russian models

Taking part in a meat raffle

Trying to pay with an American Express Card

Spending May Day anywhere other than Homebase

Expressing an opinion about absolutely anything in the street WhatsApp group

Foraging for wild garlic on National Trust property

Clapping when the plane lands

Holding a large dead marlin, standing
between two bankers

Cycling without a helmet and at least
one Day-Glo piece of clothing

Doing a nightclub PA courtesy of
Hawaiian Tropic

Hanging an arm out of a van window

Ordering a steak slice from Greggs
wearing paint-splattered jeans

Walking either a Staffordshire Bull Terrier
or any number of Corgis

Paying a family from Albania to
wash the car

Posing next to any animal that anyone has
just shot (except a werewolf)

Vaping in the doorway of a Betfred

Pigeon fancying. Or racing. Or just
letting them stand on his head while
he feeds them

Opening a toughened-glass floor panel that leads down a spiral staircase to a temperature-controlled wine cellar that he saw advertised in the *FT*'s How to Spend It supplement

Keeping coal in the bath

Warming his hands over a fire in hole-ridden metal bin wearing a donkey jacket

Joining a brass band *or* operatic society

Paving over a front garden

Commissioning a portrait of the family

Having any sort of presence on Etsy

Wiping the tears from his eyes whilst listening to Wagner

Wearing a cravat at Wimbledon

Reading a brochure for an indoor swimming pool

Making tea from a Verana boiling water tap

Mounting any part of a lion on a wall

Making a child hold a witty placard
on a march

Presenting Sir Cliff Richard with a
lifetime achievement award

Wearing a *Peaky Blinders* hat (or any
Stone Island clothing)

Wearing a Hugo Boss suit

Or any sort of armband

Or any form of jackboot

Or epaulette

Or a medal

Or a monocle

Or a shell suit

Or a novelty cardboard Ali G mask

And Finally

Ncone of us planned to turn into who we have become in middle age, but everybody picks a lane in the end. Centrist Dad just picked the middle one. And now he's there, he's just trying to at least maintain a speed that doesn't put the people around him in imminent danger and send vape plumes out of the window at the lights. Life is steady for Centrist Dad. Just as long as he doesn't lose his balance.

After all, perching on that fence isn't easy. Nor is it comfortable. It is, in fact, a pain in the arse. But so are haemorrhoids, and he's used to them, and they don't have the clear advantage of being mercifully metaphorical.

Luckily, sitting on the fence is also just like riding a bike, and Centrist Dad aces that. It uses the same set of skills, but doesn't require the Spandex, the isotonic drink, or a shower afterwards. (And he could probably get 100 panels of that fencing for the price of his 12-speed Trek.)

Centrist Dad probably used to think of himself as a bastion of openness and common sense, who's often correct. And that's probably who he was. And possibly who he still is. But, with time and some honest reflection, he has come to realise that he's more than that. He's also slightly irritating and unlikely to bring any meaningful change to the world.

But, hey – at least he's not a boringly righteous culture warrior or a frothing internet swivel-eye. They may change the world, but probably only by ramping up their unpopularity and their ever-climbing blood pressure. They're headed for irrelevance and beta blockers. Centrist Dad

If cycling down the middle of the road forever is wrong, Centrist Dad doesn't want to be right.

is headed for the Decathlon summer sale. And he's coming back with a whole new thermal base layer, baby, and you'd better believe it.

The last step on the road to being fully at one with his centrism is for Centrist Dad to take comfort in his carefully engineered position. If he can do this, he can learn to relax on that fence, like it was some Zen arse workout that let his bum unwind.* At this point, Centrist Dad, unlike football, is coming home.

Now he's in the Kübler-Ross acceptance phase of his centrism, Centrist Dad is making peace with what he is. He's a mild curry. He's a sensible shirt. He's a Sports Direct mug. He's 12pt Arial. He's an off-white paint. He's a Richard Osman novel. He's a fortnight in Brittany. He's a Nationwide current account. He's 'wash at 30°C'. He's a pair of readers from Specsavers. He's a hydrangea. He's a Yamaha guitar. He's two scoops of ice cream. He's a 5W LED bulb. He's a room in the Premier Inn. He's recycled wrapping paper. He's carrot cake. He's a Dustbuster for the crumbs. He's a hit by The Lightning Seeds. He's Factor 30. He's a Berghaus waterproof. He's the fourth row of the balcony. He's Any Other Business. He's neat reverse parking.

---

* As in 'untangle,' not as in 'rid itself of air'.

He's spreadsheets. He's semi-skimmed. He's polite applause. He's 'don't rock the boat'. He's 'mustn't grumble'. He's 'that'll do'. He's … *you*.

You are Centrist Dad. Embrace your mighty powers, O towering giant of moderation. Others will look upon your really very reasonable decisions and weep. They will kneel at your carefully balanced two feet as you bestride all opinion.

You have arrived at your superbeige self, Centrist Dad. This is your moment. Throw those curtains wide. Go forward in balance and peace. And remember: nobody, not even you, is right about everything all the time. Or wrong. But in the land of Yes and No, the man with the golden Maybe is king.

DON'T LEAVE REPUTATIONAL BIN FIRE INSURANCE UNTIL IT'S TOO LATE!

GET A QUOTE FOR CANCEL COVER NOW!

It's the nightmare that every Centrist Dad fears more than anything else in the world: *GETTING CANCELLED.*

You've spent years trying to say the least offensive thing in every situation, but now the discourse is going faster than your ability to keep up with the latest #hashtags, hot takes and woke tripwires.

You unwittingly make a clumsy faux pas online and they come for you from all angles. Your pink-haired teenage children retreat to their bedrooms with shame, and Racist Geoff off Facebook calls you a Centurion at the Gates of Free Speech.

Your boss calls you in and tells you that from now on as far as he is concerned you no longer exist.

You have been CANCELLED.

CANCEL COVER is an insurance policy for Centrist Dads that gives you peace of mind if you accidentally swerve off the road into the ditch of modern discourse and find yourself culturally cancelled. When the online hate-mobs descend on you from all sides and the rest of your family refuse to talk to you, Cancel Cover will be there for you.

In the event that your job should become instantly untenable even though you didn't mean to offend anyone, our tax-free cash policy will give you one less thing to worry about, so you can keep your head down for a while and start to rebuild your life again.

NOT TO SCARE YOU BUT DID YOU KNOW . . .

- **Around 1.4 million Centrist Dads a day are saying things in meetings that are casually upholding Patriarchal Structures.**

- **One in two Centrist Dads haven't realised that joking about identifying as an inanimate object will stop people from inviting them for work drinks.**

- **67% of Centrist Dads say they would STILL consider telling people that they find Ricky Gervais's stand-up 'refreshing'. It isn't!**

- **Trying to get a new career going after being rejected by THE ENTIRE INTERNET is like trying to push porridge up a mountain.**

Even an innocuous comment or a retweeted joke made by SOMEBODY WHO ISN'T YOU back in 2009 is now grounds to ignore everything good you have ever said and done.

OK I GET IT. WHAT WILL I BE COVERED FOR?

- Accidental pronoun lapse
- Misjudged use of phrase from 90s lads' mag
- Failure to remove J. K. Rowling books from spare room
- Making a clumsy observation about female football commentators
- Flying the national flag upside down
- Joining in with too many of the lyrics of a rap
- Repeating something heard on GB news ... *and much more*

BENEFITS

- Up to twelve months' salary for when you can't get hired for shit anymore
- 20% Discount on Family Therapy until your kids are speaking to you again
- Faceless spokesperson willing to read out your press release in public
- 30 days' FREE use of luxury 'villa' in Clacton while it all settles down
- First two hours FREE with our carefully worded apology coach
- 10% off your DIVORCE if your partner files within a week of your dickheadedness

---

BUT ISN'T CANCELLATION COVER JUST FOR FAMOUS PEOPLE?

This is a very common misconception. The Truth is **IT CAN HAPPEN TO ANYONE!** Take a look at these **genuine testimonials** from ordinary Centrist Dads.

CANCEL COVER saved my career after circumstances aligned to make me look like I had been an arsehole to a waiter in a fancy restaurant. Which I absolutely hadn't, though I apologised.
— James C.

If it wasn't for CANCEL COVER I'm not sure anyone in my industry would still want to work with me after dedicating several years of my life being perceived to be needlessly dying on a hill at the reactive core of a well-known divisive social media topic. Thank you!
— Graham L.

After years of presenting as a moody liberal teenager, the world at large suddenly and wrongly arrived at the conclusion that I am now a borderline fascist curmudgeon with no heart. Only CANCEL COVER truly understands me.
— Steven M.

Thanks to CANCEL COVER I have been able to concentrate on tweeting swastikas, calling people paedophiles and blacking up, whilst the career I was previously known for dies in the bin. Best £60 per month I have ever spent!
— Laurence F.

www.cancelcover.co.uk

Image Credits

p. viii: Middle-aged man listening to music © Mix and Match Studio/500px/Getty; p4: Man working in cafe on laptop looking pleased with himself © Mix and Match Studio/Shutterstock; p. 12: Gareth Southgate at the UEFA Euro 2024 final © Dan Mullan/Staff/Getty; p. 21: Keir Starmer at Olympic Games 2024 © Karwai Tang/Getty; p. 23: Man relaxing with question mark © David Lees/Getty; p. 29: Father and daughter wearing robot costumes © MoMo Productions/Getty; p. 40: Father doing a puzzle with his children © MoMo Productions/Getty; p. 49: Man in wireless headphones walking down the street © Oleg Elkov/Shutterstock; p. 57: Folding bikes race at Goodwood © Matthew Lloyd/Stringer/Getty; p. 61: Smiling man outdoors © Monkey Business Images/Shutterstock; p. 65: Susanna Reid at RHS Chelsea Flower Show © Karwai Tang/Getty; p. 65: Chicken tikka masala © Jack7_7/Shutterstock; p. 69: Human and monkey evolution © David Carillet/Shutterstock; p. 72: Paul Gascoigne cries © David Cannon/Getty; p. 75: Pesto pasta © Annabelle Breakey/